THE COMMERCIAL COURT GUIDE

THE COMMERCIAL COURT GUIDE
10th Edition 2018

(Incorporating The Admiralty Court Guide)

With

The Financial List Guide

The Circuit Commercial (Mercantile) Court Guide

Edited by the Judges of the Commercial Court of England & Wales

10th edition published 2018
by Informa Law from Routledge
2 Park Square, Milton Park, Abingdon, Oxon OX14 4RN

And by Informa Law from Routledge
711 Third Avenue, New York, NY 10017

Informa Law from Routledge is an imprint of the Taylor & Francis Group, an informa business

© Crown Copyright 2018

The right of The Judges of the Commercial Court to be identified as author of this work has been asserted by them in accordance with sections 77 and 78 of the Copyright, Designs and Patents Act 1988.

All rights reserved. No part of this book may be reprinted or reproduced or utilised in any form or by any electronic, mechanical, or other means, now known or hereafter invented, including photocopying and recording, or in any information storage or retrieval system, without permission in writing from the publishers.

Whilst every effort has been made to ensure that the information contained in this book is correct, neither the author nor Informa Law can accept any responsibility for any errors or omissions or for any consequences arising therefrom.

Trademark notice: Product or corporate names may be trademarks or registered trademarks, and are used only for identification and explanation without intent to infringe.

British Library Cataloguing-in-Publication Data
A catalogue record for this book is available from the British Library

Library of Congress Cataloging-in-Publication Data
Names: Great Britain. Commercial Court.
Title: The commercial court guide : (incorporating the admiralty court guide) with the financial list guide, the circuit commercial (mercantile) court guide / edited by the Judges of the commercial court of England & Wales.
Description: 10th edition. | Abingdon, Oxon [UK] ; New York, NY : Informa Law from Routledge, 2018.
Identifiers: LCCN 2018014679 (print) | LCCN 2018015232 (ebook) | ISBN 9780429456060 (ebk) | ISBN 9781138315563 (pbk)
Subjects: LCSH: Commercial courts—England. | Commercial courts—Wales.
Classification: LCC KD7182 (ebook) | LCC KD7182 .C659 2018 (print) | DDC 346.4207/0269—dc23
LC record available at https://lccn.loc.gov/2018014679

ISBN: 978-1-138-31556-3 pbk
eISBN: 978-0-429-45606-0 ebk

Typeset in Gill Sans
by Apex CoVantage, LLC.

CONTENTS

Part 1

The Commercial Court Guide

Introduction   3

Section A   Preliminary

1. The procedural framework   7
2. The Admiralty & Commercial Registry; the Commercial Court Listing Office   8
3. The Commercial Court Users Committee   9
4. Specialist associations   9

Section B   Commencement, Transfer and Removal

1. Commercial cases   10
2. Starting a case in the Commercial Court, and Electronic Working (CE File)   11
3. Pre-Action Protocols   11
4. Part 7 claims   12
5. Part 8 claims   14
6. Part 20 claims   15
7. Service of the claim form   15
8. Service of the claim form out of the jurisdiction   16
9. Acknowledgment of service   16
10. Disputing the Court's jurisdiction   17
11. Default judgment   19
12. Admissions   19
13. Transfer of cases into and out of the Commercial Court   19
14. Location of hearings before the Commercial Court   20

Contents

Section C Particulars of Claim, Defence and Reply

1	Form and content	21
2	Serving and filing particulars of claim	25
3	Serving and filing a defence	25
4	Serving and filing a reply	27
5	Amendment	28

Section D Case Management in the Commercial Court

1	Generally	29
2	Key features of case management in the Commercial Court	29
3	Fixing a Case Management Conference	32
4	Designated Judge	33
5	Case memorandum	34
6	List of Common Ground and Issues	35
7	Case management bundle	37
8	Case Management Conference	39
9	Case Management Conference: Part 8 claims	43
10	Case Management Conference: Part 20 claims (third party and similar proceedings)	44
11	Management throughout the case	44
12	Progress monitoring	45
13	Reconvening the Case Management Conference	45
14	Pre-trial checklist	46
15	Further information	46
16	Fixed trial dates	46
17	Estimates of length of trial	47
18	Pre-Trial Review and trial timetable	48
19	Orders	48

Section E Disclosure

1	Generally	53
2	Forms of disclosure order	53
3	Procedure in advance of the making of a disclosure order	55
4	Electronic Documents	56
5	Lists and disclosure statements (Standard Disclosure)	59
6	Specific disclosure	61
7	Authenticity	61

Contents

Section F Applications

1	Generally	63
2	Applications without notice	65
3	Expedited applications	66
4	Applications on documents	66
5	Ordinary applications	69
6	Heavy applications	70
7	Evidence	72
8	Reading time	73
9	Applications disposed of by consent	74
10	Hearing dates, time estimates and time limits	75
11	Application bundles	77
12	Chronologies, indices and dramatis personae	78
13	Authorities	78
14	Costs	79
15	Interim injunctions	79
16	Security for costs	83

Section G Alternative Dispute Resolution ("ADR")

1	Generally	84
2	Early neutral evaluation	86

Section H Evidence for Trial

1	Witnesses of fact	88
2	Expert witnesses	91
3	Evidence by video link	97
4	Taking evidence abroad	98

Section J Trial

1	Expedited trial; Shorter Trials Scheme; Flexible Trials Scheme	99
2	Trials of issues	99
3	Information technology at trial, including paperless trials	100
4	Documents for trial	101
5	Reading lists, authorities and trial timetable	102
6	Skeleton arguments etc. at trial	104
7	Trial sitting days and hearing trials in public	105
8	Oral opening statements at trial	105

9	Applications in the course of trial	106
10	Oral closing submissions at trial	106
11	Written closing submissions at trial	107
12	Judgment	107
13	Costs	109
14	Interest	109

Section K   After Trial

1	Continuation, variation and discharge of interim remedies and undertakings	110
2	Accounts and enquiries	110
3	Enforcement	110
4	Assessment of damages or interest after a default judgment	111

Section L   Multi-party Disputes

1	Early consideration	112
2	Available procedures	112

Section M   Litigants in Person

1	The litigant in person	114
2	Represented parties	114
3	Companies without representation	115

Section N   Admiralty

1	General	116
2	The Admiralty Court Committee	116
3	Commencement of proceedings, service of Statements of Case and associated matters	116
4	Commencement and early stages of a claim in rem	117
5	The early stages of a Collision Claim	117
6	The early stages of a Limitation Claim	119
7	E-filing	119
8	Case Management	119
9	Evidence	120
10	Split trials, accounts, enquiries and enforcement	122
11	Release of vessels out of hours	122

| 12 | Insurance of arrested property | 123 |
| 13 | Assessors | 123 |

Section O   Arbitration

1	Arbitration claims	125
	Claims under the Arbitration Act 1996	125
2	Starting an arbitration claim	125
3	The arbitration claim form	126
4	Service of the arbitration claim form	126
5	Acknowledgment of service	127
6	Standard directions	127
7	Interim remedies	128
8	Challenging the award	128
9	Time limits	132
	Claims under the Arbitration Acts 1950–1979	133
10	Starting an arbitration claim	133
11	The arbitration claim form	133
12	Service of the arbitration claim form	133
13	Acknowledgment of service	134
14	Standard directions	134
15	Interim remedies	134
16	Challenging the award	135
17	Time limits	136
	Provisions applicable to all arbitrations	136
18	Enforcement of awards	136
19	Transfer of arbitration claims	137
20	Appointment of a Commercial Judge as sole arbitrator or umpire	137

Section P   Miscellaneous

| 1 | Out of hours emergency arrangements | 138 |

Appendices

| Appendix 1 | Overriding Objective and Dedicated CPR Parts and Practice Directions | 139 |
| Appendix 2 | Case Management Information Sheet, Progress Monitoring Information Sheet and Pre-Trial Checklist | 141 |

Contents

Appendix 3	Draft ADR Order	148
Appendix 4	Standard Pre-Trial Timetable	149
Appendix 5	Preparation of Skeleton Arguments	151
Appendix 6	Preparation of Chronologies and Indices	152
Appendix 7	Preparation of Bundles (Electronic or Paper)	153
Appendix 8	Expert Evidence—Requirements of General Application	156
Appendix 9	Service out of the Jurisdiction: Related Practice	158
Appendix 10	Security for Costs: Related Practice	164
Appendix 11	Form of Freezing Order	166
Appendix 12	Electronic Working	176
Appendix 13	Electronic Track Data in Collision Claims	177
Appendix 14	Guidance on location of hearing, and on transferring cases to/from Circuit Commercial Courts	180

Addresses and Contact Details   184

Part 2

The Financial List Guide

Section A   General

1 Introduction	187
2 Jurisdiction	187
3 Financial List judges	188
4 Users' Committee	189

Section B   Procedure in the Financial List

5 CPR Part 63A and Practice Direction	190
6 Designated judges and allocation	190
7 Applicability of other procedural guides	191
8 Transfers	191
9 Market test cases	191

Section C   General Arrangements

10 Issuing proceedings in the Financial List	193

11	Arrangements for listing	193
12	Contact	193

Part 3

The Circuit Commercial (Mercantile) Court Guide

1	Introduction	197
2	Pre-action correspondence	200
3	Commencement and transfer	200
4	Communicating with the Court	205
5	Particulars of Claim, Defence and Reply	206
6	Case Management in the Circuit Commercial Court	209
7	Alternative Dispute Resolution	215
8	Applications to the court	217
9	Injunctions	221
10	Disclosure	222
11	Witness statements	225
12	Expert evidence	227
13	The pre-trial review and trial timetable	230
14	The trial	231
15	Costs	234
16	Litigants in person and companies without representation	236
17	Arbitration claims	237

Appendices

- A Court addresses and other information
- B Case Management Information Sheet
- C Specimen Directions
- D Pre-trial checklist
- E Table of cross-references

Appendices A-E may be accessed from the Circuit Commercial Court website at: https://www.gov.uk/courts-tribunals/mercantile-court

Part I
The Commercial Court Guide

Introduction

The Commercial Court; The Commercial Court Guide; The Business and Property Courts of England & Wales

The Commercial Court Guide has, like the Commercial Court itself, a long history. The Guide was last fully rewritten in 1999 alongside the introduction of the Woolf Reforms including the Civil Procedure Rules. That was, for example, before the move to the Rolls Building, and before the changes that technology has already enabled.

A number of editions of the Guide preceded and followed the 1999 edition. Many distinguished Judges of the Court have contributed over the years. In overall terms this is the tenth edition. The tenth edition does not rewrite the Guide but it does look to bring it comprehensively up to date. Revisions reflect many developments in our civil justice system. Importantly the edition continues the tradition of reflecting suggestions for improvement made by users.

The Guide is intended to promote the efficient conduct of litigation in the Commercial Court and its sister the Admiralty Court. The Guide is also used for cases in the Financial List. For cases in the Circuit Commercial Courts (the former Mercantile Courts), the Guide supplements the Circuit Commercial (Mercantile) Court Guide.

The Guide does not however provide a complete blueprint for litigation and should be seen as providing guidance to be adopted flexibly and adapted to the exigencies of the particular case. It should not be understood to override in any way the Civil Procedure Rules or Practice Directions made under them, or as fettering the discretion of the Judges.

The Commercial Court is part of the Queen's Bench Division of the High Court and within the umbrella of the Business and Property Courts of

England & Wales. Within the umbrella, the individual strengths of individual Courts remain. Commercial Court cases continue to be tried by Commercial Court Judges across banking and finance, shipping, aviation and insurance, trade, commerce and energy, and more. Its procedures and practices will continue. Its world-recognised name stays.

Alongside its work nationally, the great preponderance of the work of the Commercial Court is international. Commercial parties worldwide bring their cases to the Court through choice. English Law is a global business law as a result of choice.

The Commercial Court is also crucial to the success of the jurisdiction of England and Wales in arbitration. It is the supervisory Court supporting international arbitrations which are seated here. Because of the importance of arbitration, this aspect of the work of the Commercial Court cannot be overstated.

At the same time the Business and Property Courts umbrella adds to these individual strengths both nationally and internationally.

That collective offering is illustrated by the Rolls Building, the largest Court centre of its kind in the world. Here the Commercial Court and the Admiralty Court work collegiately with our judicial colleagues in the Chancery Division and the Technology and Construction Court. An example is the way in which Judges of the Commercial Court and the Chancery Division combine to offer the Financial List for some of the most significant financial cases. The renaming of the Mercantile Courts as Circuit Commercial Courts will emphasise the links with the Commercial Court in London. All this we hope will lead to a stronger offering for UK business nationally, including for SMEs, a vital part of our economy.

We try to keep the Guide up to date and suggestions for its improvement are always welcome. The Judges would wish to express their gratitude to all those who have made a contribution. Particular thanks are due to the following for their valued assistance: Sara Cockerill QC, Tom Ford, Joe Quinn, Daniel Hull, Dan Ward, Matthew Gaunt, Grace Karrass and Charlotte Mallorie.

On behalf of the users of the Court, and the Judges, we express our enormous appreciation to Mr Justice Knowles. He took responsibility for the rewriting of the Guide under Sir Bernard Rix as the Judge in Charge of the Commercial Court alongside the introduction of the Woolf Reforms, and he has taken responsibility for this edition. To this end, he has brought all his unrivalled experience, and we are deeply in his debt.

The Hon Mr. Justice Blair,
Judge in Charge of the Commercial Court

The Hon Mr Justice Teare,
Judge in Charge of the Admiralty Court

on behalf of the Judges of the
Commercial and Admiralty Courts

Section A
Preliminary

A1 The procedural framework

A1.1 Proceedings in the Commercial Court are governed by the Civil Procedure Rules ("CPR") and Practice Directions. References to a "Part" or to a "Rule" or to a "PD" or "Practice Direction" are to the Parts and Rules of the CPR and Practice Directions under the CPR.

A1.2 CPR Part 58 and its associated practice direction deal specifically with the Commercial Court. CPR Part 61 deals with the Admiralty Court and CPR Part 62 deals with arbitration applications. The Electronic Working Scheme applies and is dealt with by PD 51O, and see further Appendix 12.

A1.3 The Commercial Court Guide incorporates the Admiralty Court Guide. It is published with the approval of the Lord Chief Justice and the Head of Civil Justice in consultation with the Judges of the Commercial Court and the Admiralty Court and with the advice and support of the Commercial Court and Admiralty Court Users Committees. It is intended to provide guidance about the conduct of proceedings in the Commercial Court and the Admiralty Court and, within the framework of the Civil Procedure Rules and Practice Directions, to establish the practice to be followed in those Courts. Practitioners should treat the guidance as applicable to proceedings in the Admiralty Court unless the content of CPR Part 61 or section N of this Guide ("Admiralty") specifically requires otherwise.

A1.4 Financial List cases are part of the business of the Commercial Court and the Chancery Division. For matters not dealt with in the Guide to the Financial List, the Commercial Court Guide applies to cases in the Financial List.

Section A   Preliminary

A1.5   For cases in the Circuit Commercial Courts, the Commercial Court Guide supplements the Circuit Commercial (Mercantile) Court Guide.

A1.6   It is important to understand what the Guide is and what it is not. It provides guidance without prejudice to the provisions of the CPR and the Practice Directions. It is designed to serve the overriding objective (rule 1, and set out in Appendix 1). It is not itself a Practice Direction and does not constrain in any way how the Judges might exercise their discretion under the Rules and Practice Directions in accordance with the overriding objective.

A1.7   Thus, the requirements of the Guide are designed to ensure effective management of proceedings.

A1.8   Pre-trial matters in the Commercial Court and the Admiralty Court are dealt with by the Judges of those Courts: 58PD § 1.2, and not by masters or registrars.

A1.9   On matters for which specific provision is not made by the Guide, the parties, their solicitors and counsel will be expected to act reasonably and in accordance with the spirit of the Guide.

A1.10   The Court expects a high level of co-operation and realism from the legal representatives of the parties. This applies to dealings (including correspondence) between legal representatives as well as to dealings with the Court.

A.2   The Admiralty & Commercial Registry; the Commercial Court Listing Office

A2.1   The administrative office for the Admiralty Court and the Commercial Court is the Admiralty & Commercial Registry ("the Registry") which is located at 7 Rolls Building, Fetter Lane, London EC4A 1NL. The Commercial Court Listing Office ("the Listing Office") is located at the same address.

A2.2   It is important that there is close liaison between legal representatives of the parties and both the Registry and the Listing Office. All communications by one party with the Registry and/or Listing Office should be copied to other parties.

Section A Preliminary

A.3 The Commercial Court Users Committee

A3.1 The success of the Court's ability to meet the special problems and continually changing needs of the commercial community depends in part upon a steady flow of information and constructive suggestions between the Court, litigants and professional advisers.

A3.2 The Commercial Court Users Committee has assisted in this process for many years, and it is expected to continue to do so. All concerned with the Court are encouraged to make the fullest use of this important channel of communication. Correspondence raising matters for the consideration of the Committee or suggestions for changes or improvements to the Guide should be addressed to the Secretary to the Commercial Court Users Committee, 7 Rolls Building, Fetter Lane, London, EC4A 1NL or sent by email to ComCt.Listing@hmcts.gsi.gov.uk.

A3.3 The Financial List has user meetings to provide a forum in which the Court can listen and respond to matters raised by litigants and others concerned with the financial markets.

A.4 Specialist associations

A4.1 There are a number of associations of legal representatives which liaise closely with the Commercial Court and the Admiralty Court. These also play an important part in helping to ensure that the Courts remain responsive to the overriding objective.

A4.2 The associations include the Commercial Bar Association ("COMBAR"), the London Common Law and Commercial Bar Association ("LCLCBA"), the City of London Law Society ("CLLS"), the London Solicitors Litigation Association ("LSLA"), the Commercial Litigators' Forum ("CLF"), the Professional Support Lawyers Forum, the Admiralty Solicitors Group and the Admiralty Bar Group. The associations also include regional specialist associations. The Courts are also grateful for the contribution made by the Chancery Bar Association and TECBAR.

Section B

Commencement, Transfer and Removal

B1 Commercial cases

B1.1 Rule 58.1(2) describes a "commercial claim" as follows: "any claim arising out of the transaction of trade and commerce and includes any claim relating to—

- **(a)** a business document or contract;
- **(b)** the export or import of goods;
- **(c)** the carriage of goods by land, sea, air or pipeline;
- **(d)** the exploitation of oil and gas reserves or other natural resources;
- **(e)** insurance and re-insurance;
- **(f)** banking and financial services;
- **(g)** the operation of markets and exchanges;
- **(h)** the purchase and sale of commodities;
- **(i)** the construction of ships;
- **(j)** business agency; and
- **(k)** arbitration."

B1.2 Financial List claims may be issued in the Admiralty and Commercial Registry or in the Chancery Registry (PD 63A § 2.1) or transferred into that List in accordance with PD 63A § 4. Rule 63A.1 describes a "Financial List claim" as follows:
"any claim which –

(1) principally relates to loans, project finance, banking transactions, derivatives and complex financial products, financial benchmark, capital or currency controls, bank guarantees, bonds, debt securities, private equity deals, hedge fund disputes, sovereign debt, or clearing and settlement, and is for more than £50 million or equivalent;

Section B   Commencement, Transfer and Removal

(2) requires particular expertise in the financial markets; or
(3) raises issues of general importance to the financial markets."

"Financial markets" for these purposes include the fixed income markets (covering repos, bonds, credit derivatives, debt securities and commercial paper generally), the equity markets, the derivatives markets, the loan markets, the foreign currency markets, and the commodities markets.": rule 63A.1(3). The Financial Markets Test Case Scheme also operates in the Financial List: PD 51M.

B2 Starting a case in the Commercial Court, and Electronic Working (CE File)

B2.1 Except for arbitration applications which are governed by the provisions of CPR Part 62 and section O of the Guide, the case will be begun by a claim form under CPR Part 7 or CPR Part 8. Save where otherwise specified, references in this Guide to a claim form are to a CPR Part 7 claim form.

B2.2 Many documents requiring to be provided or filed are now required to be provided or filed electronically (e-filing) under the Electronic Working (CE File) arrangements which apply to the Commercial Court: see Appendix 12. An exception is available for litigants in person: see section M. The issue of any claim must, since 25 April 2017, be undertaken electronically.

B2.3 The Commercial Court may at an appropriate stage give a fixed date for trial (see section D16), but it does not give a fixed date for a hearing when it issues a claim.

B2.4 A claim in the Shorter Trials Scheme may be started in the Commercial Court: PD 51N § 2.1. The Flexible Trials Scheme applies to a claim started in the Commercial Court: PD 51N § 3.1.

B3 Pre-Action Protocols

B3.1 The Practice Direction – Pre-Action Conduct and Protocols applies to cases in the Commercial Court and usually it should be observed, although it is sometimes necessary or proper to start proceedings

Section B Commencement, Transfer and Removal

without following the procedures there contemplated: for example, where delays in starting proceedings might prompt forum-shopping in other jurisdictions. Cases in the Commercial Court are sometimes covered by an approved protocol because of the subject matter, such as the Professional Negligence Pre-Action Protocol.

B3.2 Subject to complying with the Practice Direction and any applicable approved protocol, the parties to proceedings in the Commercial Court are not required, or generally expected, to engage in elaborate or expensive pre-action procedures, and restraint is encouraged.

B3.3 Thus, the letter of claim should be concise and it is usually sufficient to explain the proposed claim(s), identifying key dates, so as to enable the potential defendant to understand and to investigate the allegations. Only essential documents need be supplied, and the period specified for a response should not be longer than one month without good reason.

B3.4 A potential defendant should respond to a letter of claim concisely and only essential documents need be supplied. It should often be possible to respond sufficiently within 21 days. A potential defendant who needs longer should explain the reasons when acknowledging the letter of claim.

B4 Part 7 claims

The form

B4.1 (a) A claimant starting proceedings in the Commercial Court must use practice form **N1(CC)** for CPR Part 7 claims.

(b) Users of the Court may from time to be asked to assist the Court with information that will enable the Court to develop appropriate statistics.

Marking

B4.2 In accordance with PD 58 § 2.3 the claim form should be marked in the top right hand corner with the words "Queen's Bench Division, Commercial Court", and on the issue of the claim form out of the Registry the case will be entered in the Commercial Court. Marking the claim form in this way complies sufficiently with PD 7A § 3.6.

Section B Commencement, Transfer and Removal

Statement of value

B4.3 Rule 16.3, which provides for a statement of value to be included in the claim form, does not apply in the Commercial Court: rule 58.5(2).

Particulars of claim and the claim form

B4.4 Although particulars of claim may be served with the claim form, this is not a requirement in the Commercial Court. However, if the particulars of claim are not contained in or served with the claim form, the claim form must contain a statement that if an acknowledgment of service is filed indicating an intention to defend the claim, particulars of claim will follow: rule 58.5(1)(a).

B4.5 If particulars of claim do not accompany the claim form they must be served within 28 days of the defendant filing an acknowledgment of service indicating an intention to defend the claim: rule 58.5(1)(c).

B4.6 The three forms specified in rule 7.8(1) must be served with the claim form. One of these is a form for acknowledging service: rule 58.5(1)(b).

Statement of truth

B4.7 (a) A claim form must be verified by a statement of truth: rule 22.1. Unless the Court otherwise orders, any amendment to a claim form must also be verified: rule 22.1(2).
(b) The required form of statement of truth is set out at PD 7A § 7.2.
(c) A claim form will remain effective even where not verified by a statement of truth, unless it is struck out: PD 22 § 4.1.
(d) In certain cases the statement of truth may be signed by a person other than the party on whose behalf it is served or its legal representative: C1.7.

Trial without service of particulars of claim or a defence

B4.8 The attention of the parties and their legal representatives is drawn to rule 58.11 which allows the Court to order (before or after the issue of a claim form) that the case shall proceed without the filing or service of particulars of claim or defence or of any other statement of case. This facility is to be used with caution. It is unlikely to be appropriate unless all the issues have already been clearly defined in

Section B   Commencement, Transfer and Removal

previous exchanges between the parties either in the course of an application before issue of claim form or in previous correspondence and then only when the issues are of law or construction.

Interest

B4.9 The claim form (and not only the particulars of claim) must comply with the requirements of rules 16.4(1)(b) and 16.4(2) concerning interest: rule 58.5(3).

B4.10 References to particulars of claim in rule 12.6(1)(a) (referring to claims for interest where there is a default judgment) and rule 14.14(1)(a) (referring to claims for interest where there is a judgment on admissions) may be treated as references to the claim form: rules 58.8(2) and 58.9(3).

B5   Part 8 claims

Form

B5.1 A claimant who wishes to commence a claim under CPR Part 8 must use practice form **N208(CC)**: PD 58 § 2.4.

B5.2 Attention is drawn to the requirement in rule 8.2(a) that where a claimant uses the CPR Part 8 procedure the claim form must state that CPR Part 8 applies. Similarly, PD 7A § 3.3 requires that the claim form state (if it be the case) that the claimant wishes the claim to proceed under CPR Part 8 or that the claim is required to proceed under Part 8.

Marking and statement of truth

B5.3 B4.2 (marking) and B4.7 (statement of truth) also apply to a claim form issued under CPR Part 8.

Time for filing evidence in opposition to a Part 8 claim

B5.4 A defendant to a CPR Part 8 claim must file an acknowledgement of service. If the defendant wishes to rely on written evidence it must file and serve that evidence within 28 days after filing an acknowledgment of service: rule 58.12.

Section B Commencement, Transfer and Removal

B6   Part 20 claims

Form

B6.1   Adapted versions of the CPR Part 20 claim form and acknowledgment of service (Practice Forms no. **N211(CC)** and **N213(CC)**) and of the related Notes for CPR Part 20 defendant have been approved for use in the Commercial Court.

B7   Service of the claim form

Service by the parties

B7.1   Claim forms issued in the Commercial Court are to be served by the parties, not by the Registry: PD 58 § 9.

Methods of service

B7.2   Methods of service are set out in CPR Part 6, which is supplemented by Practice Directions.

B7.3   PD 6A concerns service by document exchange and other means, including electronic means. There are specific provisions about when a solicitor acting for a party may be served.

Applications for extension of time

B7.4   Applications for an extension of time in which to serve a claim form are governed by rule 7.6. Rule 7.6(3)(a), which refers to service of the claim form by the Court, does not apply in the Commercial Court.

B7.5   The evidence required on an application for an extension of time is set out in PD 7A § 8.2. In an appropriate case it may be presented by an application notice verified by a statement of truth and without a separate witness statement: rule 32.6(2).

Certificate of service

B7.6   When the claimant has served the claim form the claimant must file a certificate of service: rule 6.17(2). Satisfaction of this requirement

Section B   Commencement, Transfer and Removal

is relevant, in particular, to the claimant's ability to obtain judgment in default (see CPR Part 12).

B8 Service of the claim form out of the jurisdiction

B8.1 Service of claim forms outside the jurisdiction without permission is governed by rules 6.32–6.35, and where 6.35(5) applies by PD 6B.

B8.2 Applications for permission to serve a claim form out of the jurisdiction are governed by rules 6.36 and 6.37 and PD 6B. A guide to some points of the appropriate practice is set out in Appendix 9.

B8.3 Service of process in some foreign countries may take a long time to complete; it is therefore important that solicitors take prompt steps to effect service.

B9 Acknowledgment of service

Part 7 claims

B9.1 (a) A defendant must file an acknowledgment of service in every case: rule 58.6(1). An adapted version of practice form **N9(CC)** (which includes the acknowledgment of service) has been approved for use in the Commercial Court.
(b) The period for filing an acknowledgment of service is calculated from the service of the claim form, whether or not particulars of claim are contained in or accompany the claim form or are to follow service of the claim form. Rule 9.1(2), which provides that in certain circumstances the defendant need not respond to the claim until particulars of claim have been served, does not apply: rule 58.6(1).

Part 8 claims

B9.2 (a) A defendant must file an acknowledgment of service in every case: rule 58.6(1). An adapted version of practice form **N210(CC)** (acknowledgment of service of a CPR Part 8 claim form) has been approved for use in the Commercial Court.
(b) The time for filing an acknowledgment of service is calculated from the service of the claim form.

Section B Commencement, Transfer and Removal

Acknowledgment of service in a claim against a firm

B9.3 PD 10 § 4.4 addresses acknowledgment of service where a claim is brought against a partnership.

Time for filing acknowledgment of service

B9.4   **(a)** Except in the circumstances described below, or as otherwise ordered by the Court, the period for filing an acknowledgment of service is 14 days after service of the claim form.

  (b) If the claim form has been served out of the jurisdiction without the permission of the Court under rules 6.32 and 33, the time for filing an acknowledgment of service is governed by rule 6.35, save that in all cases time runs from the service of the claim form: rule 58.6(3).

  (c) If the claim form has been served out of the jurisdiction with the permission of the Court under rule 6.36 the time for filing an acknowledgment of service is governed by rule 6.37(5), see PD 6B and the table to which it refers, save that in all cases time runs from the service of the claim form: rule 58.6(3).

B10   Disputing the Court's jurisdiction

Part 7 claims

B10.1   **(a)** If the defendant intends to dispute the Court's jurisdiction or contend that the Court should not exercise its jurisdiction it must:

    (i) file an acknowledgment of service: rule 11(2); and
    (ii) issue an application notice seeking the appropriate relief.

  (b) An application to dispute the Court's jurisdiction must be made within 28 days after filing an acknowledgment of service: rule 58.7(2).

  (c) If the defendant wishes to rely on written evidence in support of that application, it must file and serve that evidence when it issues the application. In an appropriate case it may be presented by an application notice verified by a statement of truth and without a separate witness statement: rule 32.6(2).

  (d) The parties to that application should consider at or before the time of the issue of the application or as soon as possible

Section B Commencement, Transfer and Removal

thereafter whether the application is a 'heavy application' within F6.1 likely to last more than half a day but for which the automatic timetable provisions in PD 58 § 13.2 and F6.3–F6.5 will not for any reason be appropriate. If any party considers that special timetabling is required otherwise than in accordance with those automatic provisions it should at once so inform all other parties and the Listing Office. Unless a timetable for those matters covered by F6.3 - F6.5 can be agreed forthwith, the applicant must without delay inform the Listing Office that a directions hearing will be required. For the purposes of such a directions hearing all parties must by 1pm on the day before that hearing provide to the Listing Office a brief summary of the issues of fact and law likely to arise on the application, a list of witness statements or affidavits likely to be relied upon, a list of expert evidence sought to be adduced, an estimate of how long the hearing of the substantive application will take and how much pre-hearing reading will be required by the Judge, and a proposed timetable for directions or steps leading to the hearing of the substantive application.

(e) If the defendant makes an application under rule 11(1), the claimant is not bound to serve particulars of claim until that application has been disposed of: rule 58.7(3).

Part 8 claims

B10.2 (a) The provisions of B10.1(a)–(c) also apply in the case of CPR Part 8 claims.

(b) If the defendant makes an application under rule 11, it is not bound to serve any written evidence on which it wishes to rely in opposition to the substantive claim until that application has been disposed of: rule 11(9).

Effect of an application challenging the jurisdiction

B10.3 An acknowledgment of service of a CPR Part 7 or CPR Part 8 claim form which is followed by an application challenging the jurisdiction under CPR Part 11 does not constitute a submission by the defendant to the jurisdiction: rules 11(3) and 11(7) and (8).

Section B Commencement, Transfer and Removal

B10.4 If an application under CPR Part 11 is unsuccessful, and the Court then considers giving directions for filing and serving statements of case (in the case of a CPR Part 7 claim) or evidence (in the case of a CPR Part 8 claim), a defendant does not submit to the jurisdiction merely by asking for time to serve and file a statement of case or evidence, as the case may be.

B11 Default judgment

B11.1 Default judgment is governed by CPR Part 12 and PD 12. However, because in the Commercial Court the period for filing the acknowledgment of service is calculated from service of the claim form, the reference to "particulars of claim" in PD 12 § 4.1(1) should be read as referring to the claim form: PD 58 § 6(1) and rule 58.8.

B12 Admissions

B12.1 Admissions are governed by CPR Part 14, and PD 14, except that the references to "particulars of claim" in PD 14 §§ 2.1, 3.1 and 3.2 should be read as referring to the claim form: PD 58 § 6(2).

B13 Transfer of cases into and out of the Commercial Court

B13.1 The procedure for transfer and removal is set out in PD 58 § 4. All such applications must be made to the Commercial Court: rule 30.5(3).

B13.2 Although an order to transfer a case to the Commercial Court may be made at any stage, any application for such an order should normally be made at an early stage in the proceedings.

B13.3 Transfer to the Commercial Court may be ordered for limited purposes only, but a transferred case will normally remain in the Commercial Court until its conclusion.

B13.4 An order transferring a case out of the Commercial Court may be made at any stage, but will not usually be made after a pre-trial timetable has been fixed at the Case Management Conference (see section D8).

Section B   Commencement, Transfer and Removal

B13.5 Some commercial cases may more suitably, or as suitably, be dealt with in one of the Circuit Commercial Courts or the London Circuit Commercial Court. Parties should consider whether it would be more appropriate to begin proceedings in one of those Courts and the Commercial Judge may on her or his own initiative order the case to be transferred there. Please see further Appendix 14.

B14   Location of hearings before the Commercial Court

B14.1 Cases before the Commercial Court will generally be heard in the Rolls Building in London. However, and in keeping with the Business and Property Courts initiative, if a Commercial Court hearing is more suitably held outside London the Commercial Court will aim to achieve that. And if a hearing outside London (in any Court) needs a Commercial Court Judge the Commercial Court will aim to provide a Commercial Court Judge. Please see further Appendix 14.

Section C
Particulars of Claim, Defence and Reply

C1 Form and content

C1.1 The following principles apply to all statements of case. They should, as far as possible, also be observed when drafting a CPR Part 8 claim form.

(a) The document must be as brief and concise as possible.
(b) The document must be set out in separate consecutively numbered paragraphs and sub-paragraphs.
(c) So far as possible each paragraph or sub-paragraph should contain no more than one allegation.
(d) The document must deal with the case on a point by point basis to allow a point by point response.
(e) Particular care should be taken to set out only those factual allegations which are necessary to enable the other party to know what case it has to meet. Evidence should not be included.
(f) A party wishing to advance a positive case should set that case out in the document; a simple denial is not sufficient.
(g) Where particulars are given of any allegation or reasons given for a denial, the allegation or denial should be stated first and the particulars or reasons for it listed one by one in separate numbered sub-paragraphs.
(h) Where they will assist:
   (i) headings should be used; and
   (ii) abbreviations and definitions should be established and used, and a glossary annexed.

Section C Particulars of Claim, Defence and Reply

- **(i)** Contentious headings, abbreviations and definitions should not be used. Every effort should be made to ensure that headings, abbreviations and definitions are in a form that will enable them to be adopted without issue by the other parties.
- **(j)** Particulars of primary allegations should be stated as particulars and not as primary allegations.
- **(k)** In rare cases where it is necessary to give lengthy particulars of an allegation, these should be set out in schedules or appendices.
- **(l)** A response to particulars set out in a schedule should be set out in a corresponding schedule.
- **(m)** In a rare case where it is really necessary for the proper understanding of the statement of case to include substantial parts of a lengthy document the passages in question should be set out in a schedule rather than in the body of the statement of case.
- **(n)** Contentious paraphrasing should be avoided.
- **(o)** The document must be signed by the individual person or persons who drafted it, not, in the case of a solicitor, in the name of the firm alone.

C1.2
- **(a)** A statement of case (including schedules or appendices) must not be longer than 25 pages (font minimum 12 point; 1.5 line spacing) unless the Court has given permission for a longer document, in which case it must not be longer that the increased length for which permission has been given.
- **(b)** The Court will only exceptionally give permission for a longer statement of case to be served; and will do so only where a party shows good reasons for doing so.
- **(c)** Where permission is given the Court will generally require that a summary of the statement of case is also served.
- **(d)** Any application to serve a statement of case longer than 25 pages should be made on documents (i.e. without a hearing) briefly stating the reasons for exceeding the 25 page limit and specifying the length of statement of case said to be necessary and (unless there is good reason otherwise) attaching the draft statement of case for which permission is sought.

C1.3
- **(a)** Particulars of claim, the defence and also any reply must comply with the provisions of rules 16.4 and 16.5, save that rules 16.5(6) and 16.5(8) do not apply.
- **(b)** The requirements of PD 16 § 7.4–8.1 (which relate to claims based upon oral agreements, agreements by conduct and Consumer

Section C Particulars of Claim, Defence and Reply

Credit Agreements and to reliance upon evidence of certain matters under the Civil Evidence Act 1968) should be treated as applying to the defence and reply as well as to the particulars of claim.

(c)

(i) full and specific details should be given of any allegation of fraud, dishonesty, malice or illegality; and

(ii) where an inference of fraud or dishonesty is alleged, the facts on the basis of which the inference is alleged must be fully set out.

(d) Any legislative provision upon which an allegation is based must be clearly identified and the basis of its application explained.

(e) Any provision of The Human Rights Act 1998 (including the Convention) on which a party relies in support of its case must be clearly identified and the basis of its application explained.

(f) Any principle of foreign law or foreign legislative provision upon which a party's case is based must be clearly identified and the basis of its application explained.

(g) It is important that if a defendant or CPR Part 20 defendant wishes to advance by way of defence or defence to counterclaim a positive case on causation, mitigation or quantification of damages, proper details of that case should be included in the defence or CPR Part 20 defence at the outset or, if not then available, as early as possible thereafter.

(h) Where proceedings involve issues of construction of a document in relation to which a party wishes to contend that there is a relevant factual matrix that party should specifically set out in its statement of case each feature of the matrix which is alleged to be of relevance. The "factual matrix" means the background knowledge which would reasonably have been available to the parties in the situation in which they found themselves at the time of the contract/document.

C1.4 **(a)** PD 16 § 7.3 relating to a claim based upon a written agreement should be treated as also applying to the defence, unless the claim and the defence are based on the same agreement.

(b) In many cases attaching documents to or serving documents with a statement of case does not promote the efficient conduct of the proceedings and should be avoided.

Section C Particulars of Claim, Defence and Reply

- **(c)** If documents are to be served at the same time as a statement of case they should normally be served separately from rather than attached to the statement of case.
- **(d)** Only those documents which are obviously of critical importance and necessary for a proper understanding of the statement of case should be attached to or served with it. The statement of case must itself refer to the fact that documents are attached to or served with it.
- **(e)** An expert's report should not be attached to the statement of case and should not be filed with the statement of case at the Registry. A party must obtain permission from the Court in order to adduce expert evidence at trial and therefore any party who serves an expert's report without obtaining such permission does so at risk as to costs.

Statement of truth

C1.5 Particulars of claim, a defence and any reply must be verified by a statement of truth: rule 22.1. So too must any amendment, unless the Court otherwise orders: rule 22.1(2); see also C5.2.

C1.6 The required form of statement of truth is as follows:

(1) for particulars of claim, as set out in PD 7A § 7.2 or PD 16 § 3.4;
(2) for a defence, as set out in PD 15 § 2.2 or PD 16 § 11.2;
(3) for a reply the statement of truth should follow the form for the particulars of claim, but substituting the word "reply" for the words "particulars of claim" (see PD 22 § 2.1).

C1.7 Rule 22.1 (6) and (8) and PD 22 § 3 state who may sign a statement of truth. For example, if insurers are conducting proceedings on behalf of many claimants or defendants a statement of truth may be signed by a senior person responsible for the case at a lead insurer, but

(1) the person signing must specify the capacity in which that person signs;
(2) the statement of truth must be a statement that the lead insurer believes that the facts stated in the document are true; and
(3) the Court may order that a statement of truth also be signed by one or more of the parties.

See PD 22 § 3.6B.

Section C Particulars of Claim, Defence and Reply

C1.8 A statement of case remains effective (although it may not be relied on as evidence) even where it is not verified by a statement of truth, unless it is struck out: PD 22 §§ 4.1–4.3.

Service

C1.9 All statements of case are served by the parties, not by the Court: PD 58 § 9.

Filing

C1.10 The statements of case filed with the Court form part of the permanent record of the Court.

C.2 Serving and filing particulars of claim

C2.1 Subject to any contrary order of the Court and unless particulars of claim are contained in or accompany the claim form:

    (a) the period for serving particulars of claim is 28 days after filing an acknowledgment of service: rule 58.5(1)(c);

    (b) the parties may agree extensions of the period for serving the particulars of claim. However, any such agreement and brief reasons must be evidenced in writing and notified to the Court: PD 58 § 7.1;

C2.2 The Court may make an order overriding any agreement by the parties varying a time limit: PD 58 § 7.2.

C2.3 The claimant must serve the particulars of claim on all other parties. A copy of the claim form will be filed at the Registry on issue. If the claimant serves particulars of claim separately from the claim form the claimant must file a copy within 7 days of service together with a certificate of service: rule 7.4(3).

C.3 Serving and filing a defence

C3.1 The defendant must serve the defence on all other parties and must at the same time file a copy with the Court.

Section C Particulars of Claim, Defence and Reply

C3.2 **(a)**
  (i) If the defendant files an acknowledgment of service which indicates an intention to defend, the period for serving and filing a defence is 28 days after service of the particulars of claim, subject to the provisions of rule 15.4(2). (See also Appendix 9 for cases where the claim form has been served out of the jurisdiction).
  (ii) If the defendant files an acknowledgement of service stating that he wishes to dispute the Court's jurisdiction and makes an application to challenge the jurisdiction within 28 days after that filing, the defendant must file and serve his written evidence in support with the application notice, but no defence need be served before the hearing of the application: see rule 11(9)).

(b) The defendant and the claimant may agree that the period for serving and filing a defence shall be extended by up to 28 days: rule 15.5(1). However, any such agreement and brief reasons must be evidenced in writing and notified to the Court: PD 58 § 7.1.

(c) An application to the Court is required for any further extension. If the parties are able to agree that a further extension should be granted, a draft consent order should be provided together with a brief explanation of the reasons for the extension, so that the matter may be dealt with on the documents.

C3.3 The general power to agree variations to time limits contained in rule 2.11 and PD 58 § 7.1 enables parties to agree extensions of the period for serving and filing a defence that exceed 28 days. However:

(a) The length of extension must in all cases be specified, and any such agreement must be evidenced in writing

(b) Where a longer extension than 28 days is being sought, then, even if the extension is agreed the Judge should be invited to make a Consent Order on documents, and the application should identify in every case any relevant forthcoming hearing date(s). If the extension sought will or may put any such hearing date at risk, the application must make that clear, as the Judge may wish to give further directions on documents or at a hearing. If the extension sought will not put any such hearing date at risk, the application should contain an express statement to that effect.

Section C Particulars of Claim, Defence and Reply

C3.4 The claimant must notify the Listing Office by letter when all defendants who intend to serve a defence have done so. This information is material to the fixing of the Case Management Conference (see D3.1).

C.4 Serving and filing a reply

C4.1 Subject to C4.3, the period for serving and filing a reply (and any accompanying defence to counterclaim) is 21 days after service of the defence: rule 58.10(1). (The period for serving a defence to counterclaim that does not accompany a reply is, in the Commercial Court, 28 days after service of the defence, in keeping with C3.2.)

C4.2 A claimant who does not file a reply does not admit what is pleaded in the defence and a claimant who files a reply that does not deal with something pleaded in the defence is not taken to admit it. A reply should be served only when necessary and then only plead what is necessary: it should not repeat what is pleaded in the particulars of claim.

C4.3 (a) A reply must be filed at the same time as it is served: rule 15.8(b); rule 15.8(a) does not apply in proceedings in the Commercial Court.

(b) The reply should be served before case management information sheets are provided to the Court (see D8.5). In the normal case, this will allow the parties to consider any reply before completing the case management information sheet, and allow time for the preparation of the case memorandum and the List of Common Ground and Issues each of which is required for the Case Management Conference (see section D5–D7).

C4.4 In some cases, more than 21 days may be needed for the preparation, service and filing of a reply. In such cases:

(a) An application should ordinarily be made on documents for an extension of time. The procedure to be followed when making an application on documents is set out in section F4.

(b) If the parties are able to agree that a further extension should be granted, a draft consent order should be provided together with a brief explanation of the reasons for the extension. The explanation should identify any relevant forthcoming hearing date(s). If the extension sought will or may put any such hearing

Section C   Particulars of Claim, Defence and Reply

date at risk, the application must make that clear, as the Judge may wish to give further directions on documents or at a hearing. If the extension sought will not put any such hearing date at risk, the application should contain an express statement to that effect.

C4.5 Any reply must be served by the claimant on all other parties: rule 58.10(1).

C.5 Amendment

C5.1 (a) Amendments to a statement of case must show the original text, unless the Court orders otherwise: PD 58 § 8.
 (b) Amendments may be shown by using footnotes or marginal notes, provided they identify precisely where and when an amendment has been made.
 (c) Unless the Court so orders, there is no need to show amendments by colour-coding.
 (d) If there have been extensive amendments it may be desirable to prepare a fresh copy of the statement of case. However, a copy of the statement of case showing where and when amendments have been made must also be made available.

C5.2 All amendments to any statement of case must be verified by a statement of truth unless the Court orders otherwise: rule 22.1(2).

C5.3 Questions of amendment, and consequential amendment, should wherever possible be dealt with by consent. A party should consent to a proposed amendment unless it has substantial grounds for objecting to it.

C5.4 Late amendments should be avoided and may be disallowed.

Section D
Case Management in the Commercial Court

D.1 Generally

D1.1 All proceedings in the Commercial Court will be subject to management by the Court.

D1.2 All proceedings in the Commercial Court are automatically allocated to the multi-track and consequently CPR Part 26 and the rules relating to allocation do not apply: rule 58.13(1).

D1.3 Except for rule 29.3(2) (legal representatives to attend Case Management Conferences and pre-trial reviews) and rule 29.5 (variation of case management timetable), CPR Part 29 does not apply to proceedings in the Commercial Court: rule 58.13(2).

D1.4 If a party has a legal representative, all Case Management Conferences must be attended by such a representative who is familiar with the case and has sufficient authority to deal with any issues that are likely to arise: rule 29.3(2).

D.2 Key features of case management in the Commercial Court

D2.1 Case management is governed by rule 58.13 and PD 58 § 10. In a normal commercial case commenced by a CPR Part 7 claim form, case management will include the following 13 key features:

(a) statements of case will be exchanged within fixed or monitored time periods;

(b) a case memorandum, a List of Common Ground and Issues and a case management bundle will be produced at an early point in the case. The parties will be expected to agree the case memorandum and the List of Common Ground and Issues;

Section D   Case Management in the Commercial Court

(c) the case memorandum, List of Common Ground and Issues and case management bundle will be amended and updated or revised on a running basis throughout the life of the case and will be used by the Court at every stage of the case. In particular the List of Common Ground and Issues will be used as a tool to define what factual and expert evidence is necessary and the scope of disclosure;

(d) the Court itself will approve the List of Common Ground and Issues and may require the further assistance of the parties and their legal representatives in order to do so;

(e) a mandatory Case Management Conference will be held shortly after statements of case have been served, if not before (and preceded by the parties filing case management information sheets identifying their views on the requirements of the case);

(f) at the Case Management Conference the Court will (as necessary) discuss the issues in the case and the requirements of the case with the advocates retained in the case. In a case where expert evidence is proposed the Court will consider whether to grant permission for that evidence and how that evidence should be controlled. The Court will set a pre-trial timetable and give any other directions as may be appropriate;

(g) after statements of case have been served, each of the parties may serve a disclosure report (see further E2.3). At the first Case Management Conference, the Court will discuss with the advocates retained in the case, and by reference to the List of Common Ground and Issues, the strategy for disclosure with a view to ensuring that disclosure is addressed in accordance with section E;

(h) before the progress monitoring date the parties will report to the Court, using a progress monitoring information sheet, the extent of their compliance with the pre trial timetable;

(i) on or shortly after the progress monitoring date a Judge may (without a hearing) consider progress and give such further directions as she or he thinks appropriate;

(j) if at the progress monitoring date all parties have indicated that they will be ready for trial, all parties will complete a pre-trial checklist;

(k) in appropriate cases the Case Management Conference will be restored and/or there will be a pre-trial review;

(l) the parties will be required to prepare a trial timetable for consideration by the Court;

Section D   Case Management in the Commercial Court

(m) throughout the case there must be regular reviews of the estimated length of trial, including how much pre-trial reading should be undertaken by the Judge.

D2.2 The parties should consider, ordinarily before proceedings commence or at least in advance of the first Case Management Conference, whether a case is suitable for the Shorter Trials Scheme or the Flexible Trials Scheme in the interest of reducing the length and cost of trial: PD 51N. For example the parties may be able to agree (subject to the Court) to confine matters (including the time allowed to each party at trial) so that a case which might ordinarily take longer at trial can be tried in a shorter period under the Shorter Trials Scheme.

D2.3 The Costs Management section of CPR Part 3 and PD 3E applies to all Admiralty and Commercial Court claims commenced on or after 22 April 2014 except where the claim is stated or valued at £10 million or more or where the Court otherwise orders. Save in such cases the parties will be required to file and exchange costs budgets in accordance with rules 3.12 and 3.13. If there is a disagreement between the parties as to the value of the claim, the matter should be discussed between the parties with a view to resolving the point by agreement and otherwise raised with the Court at the first opportunity (which may be the first Case Management Conference); the requirements for filing and exchanging costs budgets will not apply until the matter is resolved.

D2.4 **(a)** Unless an earlier costs management conference has been convened the issue of costs budgeting and whether a costs management order should be made will be considered at the first Case Management Conference. Parties should consider the need for costs budgets.

(b) The Court encourages input from users as to the best ways of implementing costs budgeting and costs management in the wide variety of cases heard by the Court.

(c) Where costs budgets are needed but cannot be determined in advance of directions at the Case Management Conference, then a separate Costs Management Conference may be scheduled if the parties cannot agree a budget in the light of the Court's directions.

Section D   Case Management in the Commercial Court

D.3 Fixing a Case Management Conference

D3.1 A mandatory Case Management Conference will normally take place on the first available date 6 weeks after all defendants who intend to serve a defence have done so. This will normally allow time for the preparation and service of any reply (see section C4).

D3.2 (a) If proceedings have been started by service of a CPR Part 7 claim form, the claimant must take steps to fix the date for the Case Management Conference with the Listing Office in co-operation with the other parties within 14 days of the date when all defendants who intend to file and serve a defence have done so: PD 58 § 10.2(a). The parties should bear in mind the need to allow time for the preparation and service of any reply.

(b) If proceedings have been begun by service of a CPR Part 8 claim form, the claimant must take steps to fix a date for the Case Management Conference with the Listing Office in co-operation with the other parties within 14 days of the date when all defendants who wish to serve evidence have done so: PD 58 § 10.2(b).

D3.3 (a) In accordance with section C3 the Registry will expect a defence to be served and filed by the latest of:

(i) 28 days after service of particulars of claim (as certified by the certificate of service); or
(ii) any extended date for serving and filing a defence as notified to the Court in writing following agreement between the parties; or
(iii) any extended date for serving and filing a defence as ordered by the Court on an application.

(b) If within 28 days after the latest of these dates has passed for each defendant, the parties have not taken steps to fix the date for the Case Management Conference, the Listing Office may inform the Judge in Charge of the Commercial Court, and if he or she directs will take steps to fix a date for the Case Management Conference without further reference to the parties.

D3.4 If the proceedings have been transferred to the Commercial Court, the claimant must apply for a Case Management Conference within 14 days of the date of the order transferring them, unless the Judge held, or gave directions for, a Case Management Conference when he made the order transferring the proceedings: PD 58 § 10.3.

D3.5 If the claimant fails to make an application as required by the rules, any other party may apply for a Case Management Conference: PD 58 § 10.5.

D3.6 (a) In some cases it may be appropriate for a Case Management Conference to take place at an earlier date.

(b) Any party may apply to the Court in writing at an earlier time for a Case Management Conference: PD 58 § 10.4. A request by any party for an early Case Management Conference should be made in writing to the Judge in Charge of the Commercial Court, on notice to all other parties, at the earliest possible opportunity.

D3.7 If before the date on which the Case Management Conference would be held in accordance with this section D3 there is a hearing in the case at which the parties are represented, the business of the Case Management Conference will normally be transacted at that hearing and there will be no separate Case Management Conference.

D3.8 The Court may fix a Case Management Conference at any time on its own initiative. If it does so, the Court will normally give at least 7 days notice to the parties: PD 58 § 10.6.

D3.9 A Case Management Conference may not be postponed or adjourned without an order of the Court.

D.4 Designated Judge

D4.1 An application for the appointment of a designated Judge to a case may be made in circumstances where any or all of the following factors make it appropriate:

(a) the particular size of or complexity of the case,

(b) the fact that the case has the potential to give rise to numerous pre-trial applications,

(c) there is a likelihood that specific assignment will give rise to a substantial saving in costs,

(d) the same or similar issues arise in other cases,

Section D Case Management in the Commercial Court

(e) other case management considerations indicate that assignment to a specific Judge at the start of the case, or at some subsequent date, is appropriate.

D4.2 An application for the appointment of a designated Judge should be made in writing to the Judge in Charge of the Commercial Court at the time of fixing the Case Management Conference. In appropriate cases the Court may appoint a designated Judge regardless of whether an application is made.

D4.3 If an order is made for appointment of a designated Judge, the designated Judge will preside at all subsequent pre-trial Case Management Conferences and other hearings. Normally all applications in the case, other than applications for an interim payment, will be determined by the designated Judge and she or he will be the trial Judge.

D4.4 Even where no designated Judge is appointed, in all cases the Commercial Court Listing office will endeavour to ensure a degree of judicial continuity. To assist in this, where a previous application in the case has been determined by a Judge of the Commercial Court whether at a hearing or on documents, the parties should indicate clearly when providing the documents, the identity of the Judge who last considered the matter, so that so far as reasonably practicable, the documents can be placed before that Judge.

D4.5 In deciding whether to appoint a designated Judge, the Judge in Charge of the Commercial Court will, in accordance with the overriding objective, consider the implications for other users in other cases.

D4.6 Proceedings in the Financial List will have a designated Judge assigned to them at the time of the first Case Management Conference.

D.5 Case memorandum

D5.1 In order that the Judge conducting the Case Management Conference may be informed of the general nature of the case and the issues which are expected to arise, after service of the defence and any reply the solicitors and counsel for each party shall draft an agreed case memorandum. Experience has shown that this document is very useful to the Court.

Section D Case Management in the Commercial Court

D5.2 The case memorandum should contain:

(a) a short and uncontroversial description of what the case is about; and

(b) a very short and uncontroversial summary of the material procedural history of the case.

D5.3 Unless otherwise ordered, the solicitors for the claimant are to be responsible for producing and filing the case memorandum, and where appropriate for revising it.

D5.4 The case memorandum should not refer to any application for an interim payment, to any order for an interim payment, to any voluntary interim payment, or to any payment or offer under CPR Part 36 or CPR Part 37.

D5.5 (a) The purpose of the case memorandum is to help the Judge understand broadly what the case is about. It does not play any part in deciding issues at the trial. It is unnecessary, therefore, for parties to be unduly concerned about the precise terms in which it is drafted, provided it contains a reasonably fair and balanced description of the case. The parties must do their best to spend as little time as practicable in drafting and negotiating the wording of the memorandum and keep clearly in mind the need to limit costs.

(b) Accordingly, in most cases it should be possible for the parties to draft an agreed case memorandum. However, if it proves impossible to do so, the claimant must draft the case memorandum and send a copy to the defendant. The defendant may provide its comments to the Court (with a copy to the claimant) separately.

(c) The failure of the parties to agree a case memorandum is a matter which the Court may wish to take into account when dealing with the costs of the Case Management Conference.

D.6 List of Common Ground and Issues

D6.1 (a) After service of the defence (and any reply), the solicitors and counsel for each party shall produce a list of the key issues in the case. The list should include the main issues of both fact and law. The list should identify the principal issues in a structured

Section D Case Management in the Commercial Court

manner, such as by reference to headings or chapters. Long lists of detailed issues should be avoided, and sub-issues should be identified only when there is a specific purpose in doing so.

(a) The beginning section of the document must specify what is common ground between the parties. This is an important part of the process, intended to cut down the areas in dispute and save costs.

(b) The common ground section should include features of the factual matrix which are agreed to be relevant. Any disagreements as to the relevant features of the factual matrix should be addressed in the List of Common Ground and Issues.

D6.2 (a) The List of Common Ground and Issues is intended to be a neutral document for use as a case management tool at all stages of the case by the parties and the Court. Neither party should attempt to draft the list in terms which advance one party's case over that of another.

(b) It is unnecessary, therefore, for parties to be unduly concerned about the precise terms in which the List of Common Ground and Issues is drafted, provided it presents the structure of the case in a reasonably fair and balanced way. Above all the parties must do their best to spend as little time as practicable in drafting and negotiating the wording of the List of Common Ground and Issues and keep clearly in mind the need to limit costs.

(c) Accordingly, in most cases it should be possible for the parties to draft an agreed List of Common Ground and Issues, and for that list to be concise. However, if it proves impossible to draft an agreed list, the claimant must draft the list and send a copy to the defendant. The defendant may provide its comments or mark amendments to the list and send a copy to the claimant.

D6.3 (a) The List of Common Ground and Issues at least in draft is to be available to the Court prior to the first Case Management Conference. It is intended that at that stage the list should be in a general form, identifying the key issues and the structure of the parties' contentions, rather than setting out all detailed sub-issues.

(b) At the first Case Management Conference and any subsequent Case Management Conferences which take place, the Court will review the draft List of Common Ground and Issues with a view to its being refined and identifying the importance of any sub-issues and as required in order to manage the case. Accordingly the List of Common Ground and Issues may be developed, by expansion or reduction as the case progresses.

D6.4 The List of Common Ground and Issues will be used by the Court and the parties as a case management tool as the case progresses to determine such matters as the scope of disclosure and of factual and expert evidence and to consider whether issues should be determined summarily or preliminary issues should be determined.

D6.5 The List of Common Ground and Issues is a tool for case management purposes and is not intended to supersede the pleadings which remain the primary source for each party's case. If at any stage of the proceedings, any question arises as to the accuracy of the List of Common Ground and Issues, it will be necessary to consult the statements of case, in order to determine what issues arise.

D.7 Case management bundle

Preparation

D7.1 Before the Case Management Conference (see sections D3 and D8), a case management bundle should be prepared by the solicitors for the claimant: PD 58 § 10.8.

Contents

D7.2 The case management bundle should contain the documents listed below (where the documents have been created by the relevant time):

(a) the claim form;
(b) all statements of case (excluding schedules), except that, if a summary has been prepared, the bundle should contain the summary, not the full statement of case;
(c) the case memorandum (see section D5);
(d) the List of Common Ground and Issues (see section D6);
(e) the case management information sheets and the pre-trial timetable if one has already been established (see D8.5 and D8.10);

(f) the principal orders in the case;
(g) any agreement in writing made by the parties to disclose documents without making a list or any agreement in writing that disclosure (or inspection or both) shall take place in stages.

See generally PD 58 § 10.8.

D7.3 It is also useful for the case management bundle to include any disclosure reports or questionnaires.

D7.4 The case management bundle should not include a copy of any order for an interim payment.

Providing the case management bundle

D7.5 (a) The case management bundle should be provided to the Listing Office at least 7 days before the (first) Case Management Conference (or earlier hearing at which the parties are represented and at which the business of the Case Management Conference may be transacted: see D3.7)

(b) The case management bundle (including the Case Memorandum and the List of Common Ground and Issues) must thereafter be provided at all subsequent hearings in the case and in accordance with the timetable requirements for providing bundles set out in this Guide.

(c) In a case in which costs management applies, budgets in the form of Precedent H under the CPR should be provided at the same time as the case management bundle and as part of it.

(d) In general (unless the Court otherwise orders) the case management bundle prepared for the Court will be returned to the claimant's solicitors after each hearing.

Preparation and upkeep

D7.6 The claimant (or other party responsible for the preparation and upkeep of the case management bundle), in consultation with the other parties, must revise and update the case management bundle as the case proceeds: PD 58 § 10.9.

D.8 Case Management Conference

Application to postpone the Case Management Conference

D8.1   **(a)**   An application to postpone the Case Management Conference must be made within 21 days after all defendants who intend to serve a defence have done so.

        (b)   The application will be dealt with on documents unless the Court considers it appropriate to direct an oral hearing.

Attendance at the Case Management Conference

D8.2   Clients need not attend a Case Management Conference unless the Court otherwise orders. A representative who has conduct of the case must attend from each firm of solicitors instructed in the case. At least one of the advocates retained in the case on behalf of each party should also attend.

D8.3   **(a)**   The Case Management Conference is a very significant stage in the case. Although parties are encouraged to agree proposals for directions for the consideration of the Court, directions will not normally be made by consent without the need for attendance.

        (b)   The general rule in the Commercial Court is that there must be an oral Case Management Conference at Court.

        (c)   However, there are cases which are out of the ordinary where it may be possible to dispense with an oral hearing if the issues are straightforward and the costs of an oral hearing cannot be justified.

        (d)   In such a case, if the parties wish to ask the Court to consider holding the Case Management Conference on documents, they must provide all the appropriate documents (see D8.3(e)) by no later than 12 noon on the Tuesday of the week in which the Case Management Conference is fixed for the Friday. That timing will be strictly enforced. If all the documents are not provided by that time, the Case Management Conference must be expected to go forward to an oral hearing. If the failure to provide the documents is due to the fault of one party and it is for that reason an oral Case Management Conference takes place, that party will be at risk as to costs.

- (e) Where a Case Management Conference is sought on documents the parties must provide the documents (which will include the case management bundle with the information sheets fully completed by each party), a draft Order and draft List of Common Ground and Issues (both agreed by the parties) for consideration by the Judge and a statement signed by each advocate:

    - (i) confirming that the parties have considered and discussed all the relevant issues and brought to the Court's attention anything that was unusual; and
    - (ii) setting out information about any steps that had been taken to resolve the dispute by ADR, any future plans for ADR or an explanation as to why ADR would not be appropriate.
    - (iii) giving a time estimate for the trial, specifically stating how much pre-trial reading by the Judge will be required.

- (f) In the ordinary course of things it would be unlikely that any case involving expert evidence or preliminary issues would be suitable for a Case Management Conference on documents. In cases involving expert evidence, the Court is anxious to give particular scrutiny to that evidence, given the cost such evidence usually involves and the need to focus that evidence. In cases where preliminary issues are sought, the Court will need to examine the formulation of those issues and discuss whether they are really appropriate.

Applications

D8.4
- (a) If by the time of the Case Management Conference a party wishes to apply for an order in respect of a matter not covered by the Questions on the case management information sheet, the application should be made at the Case Management Conference.
- (b) In some cases notice of such an application may be given in the case management information sheet itself: see D8.5(c).
- (c) In all other cases the applicant should ensure that an application notice and any supporting evidence are filed and served in time to enable the application to be heard at the Case Management Conference.

Section D Case Management in the Commercial Court

    (d) Where one or more applications are heavy applications (as described in F6) the preparation, timetabling and other arrangements for heavy applications will also apply. If a Case Management Conference in its own right, and not by reason of any applications, will require a day or more in hearing length, the parties should liaise to adjust the preparation, timetabling and other arrangements that would otherwise apply for the Case Management Conference so as to ensure that it can be conducted efficiently, and allowing adequate time for pre-reading by the Court.

Materials: case management information sheet and case management bundle

D8.5   **(a)** All parties attending a Case Management Conference must complete a case management information sheet: PD 58 § 10.7. A standard form of case management information sheet is set out in Appendix 2. The information sheet is intended to include reference to all applications which the parties would wish to make at a case management conference.

    (b) A completed case management information sheet must be provided by each party to the Court (and copied to all other parties) at least 7 days before the Case Management Conference.

    (c) Applications not covered by the standard questions raised in the case management information sheet should be entered on the sheet. No other application notice is necessary if written evidence will not be involved and the 7 day notice given by entering the application on the information sheet will in all the circumstances be sufficient to enable all other parties to deal with the application.

D8.6   The case management bundle must be provided to the Court at least 7 days before the Case Management Conference: PD 58 § 10.8.

The hearing

D8.7   The Court's power to give directions at the Case Management Conference is to be found in rules 3.1 and 58.13(4). At the Case Management Conference the Judge will:

Section D Case Management in the Commercial Court

(a) discuss the issues in the case by reference to the draft List of Common Ground and Issues, and approve a List of Common Ground and Issues;
(b) discuss the requirements of the case (including disclosure), with the advocates retained in the case;
(c) fix the entire pre-trial timetable, or, if that is not practicable, fix as much of the pre-trial timetable as possible;
(d) in appropriate cases make an ADR order;
(e) in appropriate cases, consider whether the case is suitable for the Shorter Trials Scheme or the Flexible Trials Scheme in the interests of reducing the length and cost of trial.

D8.8 At the Case Management Conference active consideration may be given, by reference to the List of Common Ground and Issues, to the possibility of the trial or summary determination of a preliminary issue or issues the resolution of which is likely to shorten the proceedings. An example is a relatively short question of law which can be tried without significant delay (though the implications of a possible appeal for the remainder of the case cannot be lost sight of). The Court may suggest the trial of a preliminary issue, but it will rarely make an order without the concurrence of at least one of the parties. Active consideration will also be given to whether any issues are suitable for summary determination pursuant to CPR Part 24.

D8.9
(a) Rules 3.1(2) and 58.13(4) enable the Court at the Case Management Conference to stay the proceedings while the parties try to settle the case by alternative means. The case management information sheet requires the parties to indicate whether a stay for such purposes is sought.
(b) In an appropriate case an ADR order may be made without a stay of proceedings. The parties should consider carefully whether it may be possible to provide for ADR in the pre-trial timetable without affecting the date of trial.
(c) Where a stay has been granted for a fixed period for the purposes of ADR the Court has power to extend it. If an extension of the stay is desired by all parties, a Judge will normally be prepared to deal with an application for such an extension if it is made before the expiry of the stay by letter from the legal representatives of one of the parties. The letter should confirm that all parties consent to the application.

(d) An extension will not normally be granted for more than four weeks unless clear reasons are given to justify a longer period, but more than one extension may be granted.

The pre-trial timetable

D8.10 The pre-trial timetable will normally include:

(a) a progress monitoring date (see section D12); and

(b) a direction that the parties attend upon the Commercial Court Listing Office to obtain a fixed date for trial.

Variations to the pre-trial timetable

D8.11 **(a)** The parties may agree minor variations to the time periods set out in the pre-trial timetable without the case needing to be brought back to the Court provided that the variation

(i) will not jeopardise the date fixed for trial;
(ii) does not relate to the progress monitoring date; and
(iii) does not provide for the completion after the progress monitoring date of any step which was previously scheduled to have been completed by that date.

(b) The Court should be informed in writing of any such agreement.

D8.12 If in any case it becomes apparent that variations to the pre-trial timetable are required which do not fall within D8.11, the parties should apply to have the Case Management Conference reconvened immediately. The parties should not wait until the progress monitoring date.

D.9 Case Management Conference: Part 8 claims

D9.1 In a case commenced by the issue of a CPR Part 8 claim form, a Case Management Conference will normally take place on the first available date 6 weeks after service and filing of the defendant's evidence. At that Case Management Conference the Court will make such pre-trial directions as are necessary, adapting (where useful in the context of the particular claim) those of the case management procedures used for a claim commenced by the issue of a CPR Part 7 claim form.

Section D Case Management in the Commercial Court

D.10 Case Management Conference: Part 20 claims (third party and similar proceedings)

D10.1 Wherever possible, any party who intends to make a CPR Part 20 claim should do so before the hearing of the Case Management Conference dealing with the main claim.

D10.2 Where permission to make a CPR Part 20 claim is required it should be sought at the Case Management Conference in the main claim.

D10.3 If the CPR Part 20 claim is confined to a counterclaim by a defendant against a claimant alone, the Court will give directions in the CPR Part 20 claim at the Case Management Conference in the main claim.

D10.4 If the CPR Part 20 claim is not confined to a counterclaim by a defendant against a claimant alone, the Case Management Conference in the main claim will be reconvened on the first available date 6 weeks after service by the defendant of the new party of parties to the proceedings.

D10.5 All parties to the proceedings (i.e. the parties to the main claim and the parties to the CPR Part 20 claim) must attend the reconvened Case Management Conference. There will not be a separate Case Management Conference for the Part 20 claim alone.

D10.6 In any case involving a CPR Part 20 claim the Court will give case management directions at the same Case Management Conferences as it gives directions for the main claim: PD 58 § 12. The Court will therefore normally only give case management directions at hearings attended by all parties to the proceedings.

D10.7 Where there is a prospect that a party to existing litigation may seek in due course to bring a related claim against other persons, but no CPR Part 20 claim is begun by the party, the matter must be raised with the Court in order that the Court can express its view as to the proper use of its resources and on the efficient and economical conduct of the litigation.

D.11 Management throughout the case

D11.1 The Court will continue to take an active role in the management of the case throughout its progress to trial. Parties should be ready at

Section D Case Management in the Commercial Court

all times to provide the Court with such information and assistance as it may require for that purpose.

D.12 Progress monitoring

Fixing the progress monitoring date

D12.1 The progress monitoring date will be fixed at the Case Management Conference and will normally be after the date in the pre-trial timetable for exchange of witness statements and expert reports.

Progress monitoring information sheet

D12.2 At least 3 days (i.e. three clear days) before the progress monitoring date the parties must each send to the Court (with a copy to all other parties) a progress monitoring information sheet to inform the Court:

(a) whether they have complied with the pre-trial timetable, and if they have not, the respects in which they have not; and

(b) whether they will be ready for a trial commencing on the fixed date specified in the pre-trial timetable, and if they will not be ready, why they will not be ready.

D12.3 A standard form of progress monitoring information sheet is set out in Appendix 2.

D12.4 The progress monitoring information sheets are, where appropriate, referred to the Judge in Charge of the Commercial Court.

D12.5 Upon considering progress monitoring information sheet, the Court may, particularly if there has been significant non-compliance with the pre-trial timetable, direct that the Case Management Conference be reconvened or require further information to be sent to the Court.

D.13 Reconvening the Case Management Conference

D13.1 In a complex case the pre-trial timetable may include provision for the Case Management Conference to be reconvened at an appropriate point. Further, if in the view of the Court the information given in the progress monitoring sheets justifies this course, the Court may direct that the Case Management Conference be reconvened.

Section D   Case Management in the Commercial Court

D13.2 At a reconvened hearing of the Case Management Conference the Court may make such orders and give such directions as it considers appropriate. Where there has been non-compliance with the pre-trial timetable, it may make such order for costs as is appropriate.

D.14   Pre-trial checklist

D14.1 Not later than three weeks before the date fixed for trial each party must send to the Listing Office (with a copy to all other parties) a completed checklist confirming final details for trial (a "pre-trial checklist") in the form set out in Appendix 2.

D.15   Further information

D15.1 (a) If a party declines to provide further information requested under CPR Part 18, the solicitors or counsel who are to appear at the application for the parties concerned must communicate directly with each other in an attempt to reach agreement before any application is made to the Court.

(b) No application for an order that a party provide further information will normally be listed for hearing without prior written confirmation from the applicant that the requirements of section D15.1(a) have been complied with.

(c) The Court will only order further information to be provided if satisfied that the information requested is strictly necessary to understand another party's case.

D15.2 Because it falls within the definition of a statement of case (see rule 2.3(1)) a response providing further information under CPR Part 18 must be verified by a statement of truth.

D.16   Fixed trial dates

D16.1 Most cases will be given fixed trial dates immediately after the pre-trial timetable has been set at the Case Management Conference.

D16.2 A fixed date for trial is given on the understanding that if previous fixtures have been substantially underestimated or other urgent matters need to be heard, the trial may be delayed. Where such delay might cause particular inconvenience to witnesses or others involved in the trial, the Commercial Court Listing Office should be informed well in advance of the fixed date.

D.17 Estimates of length of trial

D17.1 At the Case Management Conference an estimate will be made of the minimum and maximum lengths of the trial. The estimate should include time for pre-trial reading by the Judge and specify what time has been allowed for that purpose. Where, as will usually be the case, written closing submissions will precede oral closing submissions, the estimate of trial length must allow for this. The estimate will appear in the pre-trial timetable and will be the basis on which a date for trial will be fixed.

D17.2 The Court examines with particular care longer estimates, and will wish to consider with the assistance of advocates whether in the case of particularly long trials all the issues in the trial should be heard at the same hearing: see section J2.

D17.3 If a party subsequently instructs new advocate(s) to appear on its behalf at the trial, the Listing Office should be notified of that fact within 14 days. Advocates newly instructed should review the estimate of the minimum and maximum lengths of the trial, and submit to the Listing Office a signed note revising or confirming the estimate as appropriate.

D17.4 A confirmed estimate of the minimum and maximum lengths of the trial, signed by the advocates who are to appear at the trial, should be attached to the pre-trial checklist.

D17.5 It is the duty of all advocates who are to appear at the trial to seek agreement, if possible, on the estimated minimum and maximum lengths of trial.

D17.6 The provisional estimate and (after it is given) the confirmed estimate must be kept under review by the advocates who are to appear at the trial. If at any stage an estimate needs to be revised, a signed revised estimate (whether agreed or not) should be submitted by the advocates to the Commercial Court Listing Office.

Section D Case Management in the Commercial Court

D17.7 Accurate estimation of trial length is of great importance to the efficient functioning of the Court. The Court will be guided by, but will not necessarily accept, the estimates given by the parties. Save in exceptional circumstances even the most substantial and complex trial should not exceed 12 weeks in length.

D.18 Pre-Trial Review and trial timetable

D18.1 The Court will order a pre-trial review in any case in which it considers it appropriate to do so.

D18.2 A pre-trial review will normally take place between 8 and 2 weeks before the date fixed for trial, but might be earlier in particularly long or complex cases.

D18.3 Whenever possible the pre-trial review will be conducted by the trial Judge. It should be attended by the advocates who are to appear at the trial: PD 58 § 11.2.

D18.4 Before the pre-trial review or, if there is not to be one, not later than 7 days before the trial is due to commence, the parties must attempt to agree a timetable for the trial providing for oral submissions, written closing submissions (where proposed), examinations in chief (if any) and cross-examination of witnesses of fact and expert witnesses: PD 58 § 11.3. The claimant must file a copy of the draft timetable at least two days before the date fixed for the pre-trial review or the trial itself if there is no pre-trial review; any differences of view should be clearly identified and briefly explained: PD 58 § 11.4. At the pre-trial review or before or at the beginning of the trial itself if there is no pre-trial review, the Judge may set a timetable for the trial and give such other directions for the conduct of the trial as she or he considers appropriate.

D.19 Orders

D19.1 **(a)** Except for orders made by the Court on its own initiative, and unless the Court otherwise orders, every judgment or order will be drawn up by the parties and rule 40.3 is modified accordingly: rule 58.15(1).

Section D Case Management in the Commercial Court

(b) Consent orders are to be drawn up in accordance with the procedure described in section F9.

(c) All other orders are to be drawn up in draft by the parties and should, as well as being marked clearly with the word "draft":

   (i) be dated in the draft with the date of the Judge's decision;
   (ii) bear the name of the Judge who made the order (after the designation "Commercial Court");
   (iii) state (after the name of the Judge) whether the order was made in public, in private (see F1.7) or on documents.

The claimant is to have responsibility for drafting the order, unless it was made on the application of another party in which case that other party is to have the responsibility. Orders for submission to Judges, or for sealing will not be accepted without the information set out in sub-paragraphs c (i) to (iii) above.

(d) A copy of the draft, signed by the parties themselves, or by their solicitors or counsel, must be provided to the Registry **within five days** of the decision of the Court reflected in the draft, together with a further copy in Word format.

D19.2 If the Court orders that an act be done by a certain date without specifying a time for compliance, the latest time for compliance is 4.30 p.m. on the day in question.

D19.3 Orders that are required to be served must be served by the parties, unless the Court otherwise directs.

D19.4 Where the Court makes an order under rule 5.4C(4) (limiting access to a copy of a statement of case) that fact should be displayed prominently on the front of the order and all parties must inform the Commercial Court Listing Office in writing of the fact and terms of the order forthwith. It is the responsibility of the parties to obtain confirmation that the order is properly entered in the Court's filing system, and fully to bring the order to the attention of a sufficiently senior member of the Court's staff. Thereafter whenever a party files with the Court a document which is subject to such order this should be stated on the front of the document and brought to the attention of the Commercial Court Listing Office at the time of filing.

Section D Case Management in the Commercial Court

D19.5 Where the parties reach agreement that a case should be settled on the basis that the Court makes an Order for the proceedings to be stayed save for the purposes of enforcing agreed terms that are set out in a schedule or held separately (a "Tomlin" order), a copy of the agreed terms must be provided to the Court with the draft of the Order that a Judge is invited to make. The copy of the agreed terms may be provided marked "in confidence" and, once a Judge has reached a decision on whether to make the Order, may be returned to the solicitors for the parties if they are to hold the same for the future. The draft of the Order must be filed in two versions, neither dated: one must be signed on behalf of all parties and not bear the word "draft" or "minute"; the other must be in Word format.

D19.6 Where the parties seek to discontinue proceedings the following should be noted:

(a) It is not appropriate for orders to state that proceedings against one or more defendants are discontinued. The general position is that the Court has no power to order discontinuance: rule 38. Instead a claimant, in certain circumstances, is entitled to discontinue all or part of the claim.

(b) Parties considering a settlement under which use is made of that entitlement should give careful consideration to the whole of rule 38. Some, but not all, of the matters calling for consideration are referred to below.

(c) Rule 38.2(2) identifies circumstances where the Court's permission for discontinuance is required, including (a) where an interim injunction has been granted/undertakings have been given, (b) where a claimant has received an interim payment and the defendant that made the payment does not consent to discontinuance, and (c) where there is more than one claimant and the other claimants do not give written consent to discontinuance.

(d) Rule 38.6 is a default rule that the discontinuing claimant is liable for costs of the relevant defendant incurred on or before service of the notice of discontinuance. This will apply unless the Court orders otherwise.

(e) If agreement cannot be reached, applications under rule 38 should be made at a hearing unless the procedure for determination on documents in section F4 is followed.

Section D Case Management in the Commercial Court

(f) If permission to discontinue is needed and the relevant defendant consents to the grant of permission:

(1) A joint letter from both sides should explain why permission is needed, and why it is appropriate to grant permission. The letter should deal with all relevant matters including, but not limited to, identification of the specific factors which make it necessary to apply for permission, and confirmation that the parties have satisfied themselves that no other factors arise under rule 38.2. It should identify with precision what steps the parties propose to take, or what additional orders the parties seek, in order to ensure that those specific factors are adequately catered for. Thus, for example, if an injunction has been granted or an undertaking given, the proposed order might make additional provision for relevant injunction(s) and undertaking(s) to be discharged with effect from the date of the order.

(2) If the parties consider that no additional provision is needed (for example because relevant injunctions or undertakings have already been discharged), an appropriate order might be along the following lines:

"Permission is granted to the claimant to discontinue the whole of the claim against the [relevant] defendant under [if appropriate] CPR 38.2(2)(a)(i) (claims in relation to which the Court has granted an interim injunction) [and/or] CPR 38.2(2)(a)(ii) (claims in relation to which a party has given an undertaking to the Court)."

(g) Where, rather than the default rule as to costs, the parties seek a consent order under which different provision would be made:

(1) If permission to discontinue is sought, then the joint letter sent for that purpose should draw the Court's attention to the precise order as to costs which is sought in the draft order accompanying the application.

(2) If permission to discontinue is not sought, a joint letter from both sides should confirm that they have considered whether permission to discontinue is needed under rule 38.2 and have satisfied themselves that it is not.

Section D   Case Management in the Commercial Court

(3) If previous costs orders have been made, the parties should specifically discuss and agree what is to happen in relation to those orders. It will help to avoid problems later if the proposed order specifically identifies what is agreed upon.

(4) Depending upon the circumstances, an appropriate order might be along the following lines:

"Upon the claimant giving notice of discontinuance [pursuant to the permission granted in paragraph [x] above] [as regards its claim against the [relevant] defendant], CPR 38.6(1) shall not apply. Instead [IF SO AGREED: the costs order(s) dated […..] shall not be enforced and] OR [, without prejudice to costs orders already made,] there shall be no order as to the remaining costs of these proceedings."

(h) The parties should also bear in mind that if there is a counterclaim or any other type of additional claim, and it is sought to bring this to an end by discontinuance, then notice of discontinuance would need to be given by the party making the additional claim, and any order sought from the Court may need modification to take account of this.

Section E
Disclosure

E.1 Generally

E1.1 The purpose of disclosure is to assist in achieving the fair disposal and trial of a claim; the underlying principle is the promotion of the administration of justice. Regard must however be had to the overriding objective and the need to limit disclosure to that which is necessary to deal with the case justly: rule 31.5(7).

E1.2 The Court will seek to ensure that disclosure is no wider than appropriate. It will have regard to the List of Common Ground and Issues (section D6).

E1.3 The obligations imposed by an order for disclosure continue until the proceedings come to an end. If, after disclosure has been given, the existence (present or past) of further documents to which the order applies comes to the attention of the disclosing party, that party must prepare and serve a supplemental list of those documents.

E1.4 A party should always make a disclosure statement, verified by a statement of truth, to confirm it has carried out the disclosure ordered. When, as with an order for standard disclosure or otherwise, a party is required to make a reasonable search for documents the party should state in its disclosure statement any limits that it has placed upon the search on the grounds that the search would be unreasonable without the limits.

E.2 Forms of disclosure order

E2.1 The Court will wish to consider, normally at the first Case Management Conference, which of the following orders to make in relation to disclosure: rule 31.5(7)

Section E Disclosure

(1) an order dispensing with disclosure;
(2) an order that a party disclose the documents on which it relies and at the same time request any specific disclosure it requires from any other party;
(3) an order that directs, where practicable, the disclosure to be given by each party on an issue by issue basis;
(4) an order that a party give standard disclosure;
(5) an order that each party disclose any documents which it is reasonable to suppose may contain information which enables that party to advance its own case or to damage that of any other party, or which leads to an enquiry which has either of those consequences;
(6) any other order in relation to disclosure that the Court considers appropriate.

The Court may use a combination of these orders, order disclosure of one form for some of the issues and of another form for other of the issues, order sample disclosure or order disclosure in stages. It may order disclosure otherwise than by service of a list of documents, for example by service of copy documents. Rule 31.5(8) lists a number of other options.

E2.2 The reference to standard disclosure (item (4) in the menu of forms of order itemised above) is to standard disclosure as defined by rule 31.6. Standard disclosure is not a default form of order, and should not be treated as such by the parties or their legal advisers. An order for standard disclosure should be sought only where it is the most appropriate form of order from the menu of forms of order itemised above, and if it can appropriately be confined to particular issues it should be so confined. Where standard disclosure is ordered a party is required to disclose:

(a) the documents on which the party relies; and
(b) documents which—
— adversely affect the party's own case;
— adversely affect another party's case; or
— support another party's case; and
(c) documents which the party is required to disclose by any relevant practice direction.

Section E   Disclosure

E.3 Procedure in advance of the making of a disclosure order

E3.1 The provisions of rule 31.5(3)-(9) apply. In particular :

(a) Parties are expected to comply with the provisions for service of disclosure reports, and attempt to agree the ambit of disclosure in advance of the Case Management Conference.

(b) In the case of complex litigation the Court will normally be assisted by a disclosure report produced by each party, indicating (by reference to categories of documents, the location of documents and the period of time covered by the documentation and otherwise) what documentation the party recognises should be covered by disclosure, and whether the party intends to place any, and if so what, limits upon a search on the ground that the search would be unreasonable without the limits. Disclosure reports may be dispensed with if they are unnecessary or disproportionate in the particular case.

(c) Where a disclosure report is produced, the Court will normally invite the observations of other parties upon the proposals in a disclosure report with a view to determining the proper extent of disclosure and any proper limits upon the search for documents before the parties make disclosure. Disclosure reports should therefore be produced sufficiently in advance of the Case Management Conference to enable the other parties to consider their position on the proposals contained therein.

(d) Where no disclosure report is produced a statement to this effect should be in5cluded in the parties' case management information sheets. The Court will then consider with the parties at the Case Management Conference whether disclosure reports should be prepared.

E3.2 The parties should indicate in the case management information sheets the form of disclosure agreed or contended for. A party who contends that to search for a category or class of document would be unreasonable should also indicate this in the case management information sheet. Parties should be ready to assist the court with estimates of the costs of forms of disclosure order agreed or contended for.

Section E Disclosure

E.4 Electronic Documents

E4.1 All parties should have regard to issues which may specifically arise concerning electronic data and documents in accordance with PD 31B. The following is intended as indicative. The Court recognises that the technology is constantly changing, and the parties are encouraged to reach their own agreement as to how the process is to be managed efficiently.

> **(a)** Rule 31.4 contains a broad definition of "document". This extends to Electronic Documents. "Electronic Document" means any document held in electronic form. It includes, for example, e-mail and other electronic communications such as text messages and voicemail, word-processed documents and databases, and documents stored on portable devices such as memory sticks and mobile phones. In addition to documents that are readily accessible from computer systems and other electronic devices and media, it includes documents that are stored on servers and back-up systems and documents that have been deleted. It also includes Metadata and other embedded data which is not typically visible on screen or a print out.

When considering disclosure of Electronic Documents, the parties and their legal representatives should bear in mind the following general principles—

> (i) Electronic Documents should be managed efficiently in order to minimise the cost incurred;
> (ii) technology should be used in order to ensure that document management activities are undertaken efficiently and effectively;
> (iii) disclosure should be given in a manner which gives effect to the overriding objective;
> (iv) Electronic Documents should generally be made available for inspection in a form which allows the party receiving the documents the same ability to access, search, review and display the documents as the party giving disclosure; and
> (v) disclosure of Electronic Documents which are of no relevance to the proceedings may place an excessive burden in time and cost on the party to whom disclosure is given.

Section E Disclosure

(b) As soon as litigation is contemplated, the parties' legal representatives must notify their clients of the need to preserve disclosable documents. The documents to be preserved include Electronic Documents which would otherwise be deleted in accordance with a document retention policy or otherwise deleted in the ordinary course of business.

(c) The parties and their legal representatives must, before the first Case Management Conference, discuss the use of technology in the management of Electronic Documents and the conduct of proceedings, in particular for the purpose of—

   (i) creating lists of documents to be disclosed;
   (ii) giving disclosure by providing documents and information regarding documents in electronic format; and
   (iii) presenting documents and other material to the Court at the trial.

(d) The parties and their legal representatives must also, before the first Case Management Conference, discuss the disclosure of Electronic Documents. In some cases (for example heavy and complex cases) it may be appropriate to begin discussions before proceedings are commenced. The discussions should include (where appropriate) the following matters—

   (i) the categories of Electronic Documents within the parties' control, the computer systems, electronic devices and media on which any relevant documents may be held, storage systems and document retention policies;
   (ii) the scope of the reasonable search for Electronic Documents that would be required under rule 31.7 by an order for standard disclosure;
   (iii) the tools and techniques (if any) which should be considered to reduce the burden and cost of disclosure of Electronic Documents, including—

      (1) limiting disclosure of documents or certain categories of documents to particular date ranges, to particular custodians of documents, or to particular types of documents;
      (2) the use of agreed Keyword Searches;

Section E   Disclosure

(3) the use of agreed software tools;
(4) the methods to be used to identify duplicate documents;
(5) the use of Data Sampling;
(6) the methods to be used to identify privileged documents and other nondisclosable documents, to redact documents (where redaction is appropriate), and for dealing with privileged or other documents which have been inadvertently disclosed; and
(7) the use of a staged approach to the disclosure of Electronic Documents;

(iv) the preservation of Electronic Documents, with a view to preventing loss of such documents before the trial;
(v) the exchange of data relating to Electronic Documents in an agreed electronic format using agreed fields;
(vi) the formats in which Electronic Documents are to be provided on inspection and the methods to be used;
(vii) the basis of charging for or sharing the cost of the provision of Electronic Documents, and whether any arrangements for charging or sharing of costs are final or are subject to re-allocation in accordance with any order for costs subsequently made; and
(viii) whether it would be appropriate to use the services of a neutral electronic repository for storage of Electronic Documents.

(e) In some cases the parties may find it helpful to exchange the Electronic Documents Questionnaire provided for in rule 31.22 and PD 31B in order to provide information to each other in relation to the scope, extent and most suitable format for disclosure of Electronic Documents in the proceedings.

(f) The documents submitted to the Court in advance of the first Case Management Conference should include a summary of the matters on which the parties agree in relation to the disclosure of Electronic Documents and a summary of the matters on which they disagree. The person signing the Electronic Documents Questionnaire should attend the first Case Management Conference, and any subsequent hearing at which disclosure is likely to be considered.

Section E Disclosure

(g) If at any time it becomes apparent that the parties are unable to reach agreement in relation to the disclosure of Electronic Documents, the parties should seek directions from the Court at the earliest practical date. The Court will in appropriate cases resolve such issues at a Case Management Conference without a formal application being issued.

E4.2 Regard should be had to PD 31B for the detailed provisions as to the Court's approach in matters regarding electronic disclosure and the requirements of searching and listing electronic documents.

E.5 Lists and disclosure statements (Standard Disclosure)

E5.1 If an order for standard disclosure is made on one or more issues, in order to comply with rule 31.10(3) (which requires the list to identify the documents in a convenient order and manner and as concisely as possible) it may be necessary to list the documents in date order, to number them consecutively and to give each a concise description. In some cases, it will be useful to give each document a "Bates number" identifying the party disclosing it (such as C101 or D(1) 202). However, where there is a large number of documents all falling within a particular category the disclosing party may (unless otherwise ordered) list those documents as a category rather than individually.

E5.2 Each party to the proceedings must serve a separate list of documents. This applies even if two or more parties are represented by the same firm of solicitors.

E5.3 If the physical structure of a file may be of evidential value (e.g. a placing or chartering file) solicitors should make one complete copy of the file in the form in which they received it before any documents are removed for the purpose of giving disclosure or inspection.

E5.4 Unless the Court directs otherwise, the disclosure statement must comply with the requirements of rules 31.7(3) and 31.10(6). In particular, it should

(a) expressly state that the disclosing party believes the extent of the search to have been reasonable in all the circumstances; and

Section E   Disclosure

(b) draw attention to any particular limitations on the extent of the search adopted for reasons of proportionality and give the reasons why they were adopted.

E5.5 The disclosure statement for standard disclosure should begin with the following words:

"[I/we], [name(s)] state that [I/we] have carried out a reasonable and proportionate search to locate all the documents which [I am/here name the party is] required to disclose under [the order made by the Court or the agreement in writing made between the parties] on the [] day of [] 20[]."

E5.6 The disclosure statement for standard disclosure should end with the following certificate:

"[I/we] certify that [I/we] understand the duty of disclosure and to the best of [my/our] knowledge [I have/here name the party has] carried out that duty. [I/we] certify that the list above is a complete list of all documents which are or have been in [my/here name the party's] control and which [I am/here name the party is] obliged under [the said order or the said agreement in writing] to disclose."

E5.7 An adapted version of practice form **N265(CC)** (list of documents: standard disclosure) has been approved for use in the Commercial Court. The Court may at any stage order that a disclosure statement be verified by affidavit.

E5.8 (a) For the purposes of PD 31A § 4.3 the Court will normally regard as an appropriate person any person who is in a position responsibly and authoritatively to search for the documents required to be disclosed by that party and to make the statements contained in the disclosure statement concerning the documents which must be disclosed by that party.
(b) A legal representative may in certain cases be an appropriate person.
(c) An explanation why the person is considered an appropriate person must still be given in the disclosure statement.
(d) A person holding an office or position in the disclosing party but who is not in a position responsibly and authoritatively to make the statements contained in the disclosure statement will

Section E   Disclosure

not be regarded as an appropriate person to make the disclosure statement of the party.

(e) The Court may of its own initiative or on application require that a disclosure statement also be signed by another appropriate person.

E.6   Specific disclosure

E6.1 Specific disclosure is defined by rule 31.12(2). If a party believes that the disclosure of documents given by a disclosing party is inadequate it may make an application for an order for specific disclosure: PD 31A § 5.1.

E6.2 An order for specific disclosure may be directed to particular documents. An order for specific disclosure under rule 31.12 may also in an appropriate case direct a party to carry out a thorough search for any documents which it is reasonable to suppose may adversely affect the party's own case or support the case of the party applying for disclosure or which may lead to a train of enquiry which has either of these consequences and to disclose any documents located as a result of that search: PD 31A § 5.5.

E6.3 The Court may at any stage order that specific disclosure be verified by affidavit or witness statement.

E6.4 Applications for ship's papers are provided for in rule 58.14.

E.7   Authenticity

E7.1 (a) Where the authenticity of any document disclosed to a party is not admitted, that party must serve notice that the document must be proved at trial in accordance with rule 32.19. Such notice must be served by the latest date for serving witness statements or within 28 days of disclosure of the document, whichever is later.

(b) Where, apart from the authenticity of the document itself, the date upon which a document or an entry in it is stated to have been made or the person by whom the document states that it or any entry in it was made or any other feature of the

Section E Disclosure

document is to be challenged at the trial on grounds which may require a witness to be called at the trial to support the contents of the document,

(i) such challenge must be raised in good time in advance of the trial to enable such witness or witnesses to be called;
(ii) the grounds of challenge must be explicitly identified in the skeleton argument or outline submissions in advance of the trial.

(c) Where, due to the late disclosure of a document it or its contents or character cannot practicably be challenged within the time limits prescribed in (a) or (b), the challenge may only be raised with the permission of the Court and having regard to the overriding objective: rule 1.1.

Section F
Applications

F.1 Generally

F1.1 (a) Applications are governed by CPR Part 23 and PD 23A as modified by rule 58 and PD 58. As a result

  (i) PD 23A §§ 1 and 2.3–2.6 do not apply;
  (ii) PD 23A §§ 2.8 and 2.10 apply only if the proposed (additional) application will not increase the time estimate (including the estimate for the Judge's prehearing reading time) already given for the hearing for which a date has been fixed; and
  (iii) PD 23A § 3 is subject in all cases to the Judge's agreeing that the application may proceed without an application notice being served.

(b) An adapted version of practice form **N244(CC)** (application notice) has been approved for use in the Commercial Court.

F1.2 An application for a consent order must include a draft of the proposed order signed on behalf of all parties to whom it relates: PD 58 § 14.1. A further copy of the draft order must be provided in Word format. The application must also include all documents necessary for the Court to consider whether the order should be made: see further F4.1(a) and D19.5.

F1.3 The requirement in PD 23A § 12.1 that a draft order be supplied on disk does not apply in the Commercial Court: PD 58 § 14.2.

Service

F1.4 Application notices are served by the parties, not by the Court: PD 58 § 9.

Evidence

F1.5 **(a)** Attention is drawn to PD 23A § 9.1 which points out that even where no specific requirement for evidence is set out in the Rules or Practice Directions the Court will in practice often need to be satisfied by evidence of the facts that are relied on in support of, or in opposition to, the application.

(b) Where convenient the written evidence relied on in support of an application may be included in the application notice, which may be lengthened for this purpose.

Time for service of evidence

F1.6 The time allowed for the service of evidence in relation to applications is governed by PD 58 § 13.

Hearings

F1.7 **(a)** Applications (other than arbitration applications) will be heard in public in accordance with rule 39.2, save where otherwise ordered.

(b) With certain exceptions, arbitration applications will normally be heard in private: rule 62.10(3). See section O.

(c) An application without notice for a freezing injunction or a search order will often need to be heard in private in the interests of justice and therefore be heard in private: see rule 39.2(3).

F1.8 Parties should pay particular attention to PD 23A § 2.9 which warns of the need to anticipate the Court's wish to review the conduct of the case and give further management directions. The parties should be ready to give the Court their assistance and should be able to answer any questions that the Court may ask for this purpose.

F1.9 PD 23A § § 6.1–6.11 and § 7 deal with the hearing of applications by telephone (other than an urgent application out of Court hours) and the hearing of applications using video-conferencing facilities. In most cases applications not suitable to be dealt with on documents (see section F4) are more conveniently dealt with in person.

Section F Applications

F.2 Applications without notice

F2.1 All applications should be made on notice, even if that notice has to be short, unless

  (a) any rule or Practice Direction or this Guide provides that the application may be made without notice; or
  (b) there are good reasons for making the application without notice, for example, because notice would or might defeat the object of the application.

F2.2 Where an application without notice does not involve the giving of undertakings to the Court, it will normally be made and dealt with on documents, as, for example, applications for permission to serve a claim form out of the jurisdiction, and applications for an extension of time in which to serve a claim form.

F2.3 Any application for an interim injunction or similar remedy will require an oral hearing.

F2.4 **(a)** A party wishing to make an application without notice which requires an oral hearing before a Judge should contact the Commercial Court Listing Office at the earliest opportunity.
  (b) If it is essential to make an application without notice at a time when no Commercial Judge is available the party wishing to make the application should apply to the Queen's Bench Judge in Chambers (see section P1).

F2.5 On all applications without notice it is the duty of the applicant and those representing the applicant:

  (a) to make full and frank disclosure of all matters relevant to the application;
  (b) to ensure that a note or transcript of any oral hearing of the without notice application, together with the evidence and skeleton argument in support of it, all be served on the other party or parties with any order made or as soon as possible thereafter.

F2.6 The documents provided for the application should include two copies of a draft of the order sought. Save in exceptional circumstances where time does not permit, all the evidence relied upon in support of the application and any other relevant documents must be

Section F Applications

provided in advance to the Commercial Court Listing Office. If the application is urgent, the Commercial Court Listing Office should be informed of the fact and of the reasons for the urgency. The advocate's estimate of reading time likely to be required by the Court should also be provided.

F2.7 Practitioners should pay close attention to the importance of providing an accurate time estimate not only for the hearing but also for reading. In both these respects the time estimate must allow for all material that may properly need to be brought to the Judge's attention.

F2.8 Practitioners should also pay close attention to the provision of realistic reading lists. In cases of real urgency, time should be allowed in the time estimate for taking the Judge to the relevant documents, rather than asking the Judge to read everything in advance.

F.3 Expedited applications

F3.1 The Court will expedite the hearing of an application on notice in cases of sufficient urgency and importance.

F3.2 Where a party wishes to make an expedited application a request should be made to the Commercial Court Listing Office on notice to all other parties.

F.4 Applications on documents

F4.1 (a) Although contested applications are usually best determined at an oral hearing, some applications may be suitable for determination on documents submitted electronically. On any such application all documents required to determine the matter must be provided, even where the application is for an order to be made by consent. In particular:

  (i) a copy of any relevant previous order must be provided;
  (ii) an undated copy of the draft order sought should be filed in Word format;
  (iii) any order proposing to amend a directions timetable must be accompanied by a note of the trial date (or hearing date for a relevant substantive application) and confirmation

that the amendment will not affect the trial date (including any date for a pre-trial review) or hearing date for the relevant substantive application.

(b) Attention is drawn to the provisions of rule 23.8 and PD 23A § 11. If the applicant considers that the application is suitable for determination on documents, he should ensure before filing the documents with the Court

    (i) that the application notice together with any supporting evidence has been served on the respondent;

    (ii) that the respondent has been allowed the appropriate period of time in which to serve written submissions and evidence in opposition (save in cases of urgency that will ordinarily be at least three clear days);

    (iii) that any evidence in reply has been served on the respondent; and

    (iv) that there is included in the documents

        (1) the written consent of the respondent to the disposal of the application without a hearing; or

        (2) a statement by the applicant of the grounds on which he seeks to have the application disposed of without a hearing, together with confirmation that the application and a copy of the grounds for disposing of it without a hearing have been served on the respondent and a statement of when they were served.

(c) Where a previous application in the case has been determined by a Judge of the Commercial Court whether at a hearing or on documents, it is helpful for the applicant to indicate clearly when filing the documents, the identity of the Judge who last considered the matter, so that so far as reasonably practicable the documents can be placed before that Judge.

(d) A respondent served with a non-urgent application which is requested to be determined on documents should respond by letter within three clear days of the date of service on the respondent of the application, stating whether or not it consents to the application being disposed of without a hearing. If the respondent so consents it should at the same time serve any written submissions and evidence in opposition or, if

Section F Applications

further time is needed, should state how much further time is required and the grounds upon which further time is required. If the respondent does not so consent it should give reasons. The letter should be sent (by email, where possible) to the applicant and all other parties concerned in the application at the same time as it is filed with the Court.

(e) Only in exceptional cases (or where a rule specifically so provides) will the Court dispose of an application without a hearing in the absence of the respondent's consent.

F4.2 (a) Certain applications relating to the management of proceedings may conveniently be made in correspondence without issuing an application notice.

(b) It must be clearly understood that such applications are not applications without notice and the applicant must therefore ensure that a copy of the communications making the application is sent to all other parties to the proceedings.

(c) Accordingly, the following procedure should be followed when making an application of this kind:

(i) the applicant should first ascertain whether the application is opposed by the other parties;

(ii) if it is, the applicant should apply to the Court by letter stating the nature of the order which it seeks and the grounds on which the application is made and enclosing all documents required to determine the matter;

(iii) a copy of the letter should be sent (by e-mail, where possible, copied to the Court) to all other parties at the same time as it is sent to the Court and it should be stated that this has been done;

(iv) any other party wishing to make representations should do so by letter within two days (i.e. two clear days) of the date of the applicant's letter of application, unless a more prompt response is requested by or on behalf of the Court. The representations should be sent (by email where possible) to the applicant and all other parties at the same time as they are sent to the Court;

(v) the Court will advise its decision by letter or email to the applicant. The applicant must forthwith copy the Court's letter to all other parties, by email where possible;

(vi) all appropriate court fees must still be paid.

F.5 Ordinary applications

F5.1 Applications likely to require an oral hearing (i.e. oral argument) lasting half a day or less are regarded as "ordinary" applications.

F5.2 Ordinary applications will generally be heard on Fridays, but may be heard on other days. Where possible, the Listing Office will have regard to the availability of advocates when fixing hearing dates.

F5.3 **(a)** The timetable for ordinary applications (including ordinary summary judgment applications) is set out in PD 58 § 13.1 and is as follows:

  (i) evidence in support must be filed and served with the application;
  (ii) evidence in answer must be filed and served within 14 days thereafter;
  (iii) evidence in reply (if any) must be filed and served within 7 days thereafter.

(b) This timetable may be abridged or extended by agreement between the parties provided that any date fixed for the hearing of the application is not affected: PD 58 § 13.4. In appropriate cases, this timetable may be abridged by the Court.

F5.4 An application bundle (see section F11) and the case management bundle must be provided to the Listing Office by 1 p.m. one clear day before the date fixed for the hearing together with a letter from the applicant's solicitors confirming or updating the time estimate for the hearing and the reading time required for the Judge. A "clear day" is explained by rule 2.8(3). The applicant on any application must be willing to provide a copy of the application bundle and the case management bundle (and not simply an index) to other parties at the same time as those bundles are provided to the Court.

F5.5 Skeleton arguments must be provided by all parties. These must be provided to the Listing Office and served on the advocates for all other parties to the application by 1 p.m. on the day before the date fixed for the hearing (i.e. the immediately preceding day). Advocates should note:

(a) Guidelines on the preparation of skeleton arguments are set out in Appendix 5.

Section F   Applications

    (b) The skeleton should include an estimate of the reading time likely to be required by the Court and a suggested reading list.

    (c) Skeletons should not without good reason be more than 15 pages (font minimum 12 point; 1.5 line spacing) in length.

F5.6 Thus, for an application estimated for a half day or less and due to be heard on a Friday:

    (a) the application bundle and case management bundle must be provided by 1 p.m. on Wednesday; and

    (b) skeleton arguments must be provided by 1 p.m. on Thursday.

F5.7 If, for reasons outside the reasonable control of the advocate a skeleton argument cannot be delivered to the Listing Office by 1pm, the Clerk of the Judge hearing the application should be informed before 1pm and the skeleton argument should be delivered direct to the Clerk of the Judge listed to hear the application and in any event not later than 4pm the day before the hearing.

F5.8 The applicant should, as a matter of course, provide all other parties to the application with a copy of the application bundle at the cost of the receiving party. Further copies should be supplied on request, again at the cost of the receiving party.

F5.9 Problems with providing bundles or skeleton arguments should be notified to the Commercial Court Listing Office as far in advance as possible. **If the application bundle, case management bundle or skeleton argument is not provided by the time specified, the application may be stood out of the list without further warning and there may be costs consequences.**

F.6   Heavy applications

F6.1 Applications likely to require an oral hearing (ie. oral argument) lasting more than half a day are regarded as "heavy" applications.

F6.2 Heavy applications normally involve a greater volume of evidence and other documents and more extensive issues. They accordingly require a longer lead-time for preparation and exchange of evidence. Where possible the Listing Office will have regard to the availability of advocates when fixing hearing dates.

Section F Applications

F6.3 The timetable for heavy applications (including heavy summary judgment applications) is set out in PD 58 § 13.2 and is as follows:

(a) evidence in support must be filed and served with the application;
(b) evidence in answer must be filed and served within 28 days thereafter;
(c) evidence in reply (if any) must be filed and served as soon as possible, and in any event within 14 days of service of the evidence in answer.

F6.4 An application bundle (see section F11) and case management bundle must be provided to the Listing Office by 4 p.m. two days (i.e. two clear days) before the date fixed for the hearing (or, if earlier, 4 p.m. two days before the first day of the required reading period); save that if this would result in provision on a Friday then the bundles should be provided not later than 4pm on the Thursday. A "clear day" is explained by rule 2.8(3). The bundles should be provided together with a reading list and an estimate for the reading time likely to be required by the Court (see further F6.5 and F8.1) and a letter from the applicant's solicitors confirming or updating the time estimate for the hearing. The applicant on any application must be willing to provide a copy of the application bundle and the case management bundle (and not simply an index) to other parties at the same time as those bundles are provided to the Court.

F6.5 (a) Guidelines on the preparation of skeleton arguments are set out in Appendix 5.

(b) Skeleton arguments must be provided to the Listing Office and served on the advocates for all other parties to the application as follows: (i) applicant's skeleton argument (with reading list and time estimate, a chronology unless one is unnecessary, and with a dramatis personae if one is warranted), by 4 p.m. two days (i.e. two clear days) before the hearing (or, if earlier, 4 p.m. two days before the first day of the required reading period); save that if this would result in service and provision on a Friday then the skeleton argument should be provided not later than 4pm on the Thursday; (ii) respondent's skeleton argument (with reading list and time estimate), by 4 p.m. one day after the day on which the applicant's skeleton argument is required to be provided.

Section F   Applications

- **(c)** Skeletons should not be more than 25 pages (font minimum 12 point; 1.5 line spacing) in length. The Court will give permission for a longer skeleton only where a party shows good reason for doing so. Any application to serve a longer skeleton should be made on documents to the Court briefly stating the reasons for exceeding the 25 page limit and stating what number of pages are said to be necessary. Such application should be made sufficiently in advance of the deadline for service to enable the Court to rule upon it before the deadline for service. The provisions as to the length of skeletons reflect the experience of the Judges over time as to what is most useful to the Court.

F6.6 Thus, for an application estimated to require oral argument of more than half a day with an estimated reading time of 1 day and due to be heard on a Thursday:

- **(a)** the application bundle and the case management bundle and the applicant's skeleton argument must be provided by 4 p.m. on Friday;
- **(b)** the respondent's skeleton argument must be provided by 4 p.m. on Monday.

F6.7 The applicant must, as a matter of course, provide all other parties to the application with a copy of the application bundle at the cost of the receiving party. Further copies must be supplied on request, again at the cost of the receiving party.

F6.8 Problems with providing bundles or skeleton arguments should be notified to the Commercial Court Listing Office as far in advance as possible. **If the application bundle, case management bundle or skeleton argument is not provided by the time specified, the application may be stood out of the list without further warning.**

F.7   Evidence

F7.1 Although evidence may be given by affidavit, it should generally be given by witness statement, except where it can conveniently be given in the application notice (see rule 32.6(2) and except where

Section F   Applications

PD 32 requires evidence to be given on affidavit (as, for example, in the case of an application for a freezing injunction: PD 32 § 1.4). In other cases the Court may order that evidence be given by affidavit: PD 32 § 1.4(1) and 1.6.

F7.2 Witness statements and affidavits must comply with the requirements of PD 32, save that photocopy documents should be used unless the Court orders otherwise.

F7.3 (a) Witness statements must be verified by a statement of truth signed by the maker of the statement: rule 22.1.
(b) At hearings other than trial an applicant may rely on the application notice itself, and a party may rely on its statement of case, if the application notice or statement of case (as the case may be) is verified by a statement of truth: rule 32.6(2).
(c) A statement of truth in an application notice may also be signed as indicated in C1.6 and C1.7.

F7.4 Proceedings for contempt of Court may be brought against a person who makes, or causes to be made, a false statement in a witness statement (or any other document verified by a statement of truth) without an honest belief in its truth: rule 32.14(1).

F.8   Reading time

F8.1 (a) It is essential for the efficient conduct of the Court's business that the parties inform the Court of the reading required in order to enable the Judge to dispose of the application within the time allowed for the hearing and of the time likely to be required for that purpose. Accordingly:
(i) in the case of all heavy applications, each party must provide to the Listing Office together with its skeleton argument a reading list with an estimate of the time likely to be required by the Court for reading;
(ii) in the case of all other applications each party must provide to the Listing Office by 1pm on the day before the date fixed for the hearing of an application (ie the immediately preceding day) a reading list with an estimate of the time required to complete the reading;

Section F   Applications

      (iii) each reading list should identify the material on both sides which the Court needs to read.
      (iv) if possible, the parties should provide the reading list in an agreed document.

(b) Failure to comply with these requirements may result in the adjournment of the hearing.

F.9   Applications disposed of by consent

F9.1   **(a)** Consent orders may be submitted to the Court in draft for approval without the need for attendance.

      (b) Two copies of the draft, one (or a counterpart) in a form signed on behalf of all parties to whom it relates, and the other in Word format, should be filed at the Registry. The copies should be undated. The order will be dated with the date on which the Judge approves it, but that does not prevent the parties acting on their agreement immediately if they wish.

      (c) The parties should act promptly in filing the copies at the Registry. If it is important that the orders are made by a particular date, that fact (and the reasons for it) should be notified in writing to the Registry.

      (d) Where the order relates to or proposes to amend an earlier order a copy of that earlier order should also be filed at the same time.

      (e) Any consent order submitted in draft and proposing to amend a directions timetable must be accompanied by a note of the trial date (or hearing date for a relevant substantive application) and confirmation that the amendment will not affect the trial date (including any date for a pre-trial review) or hearing date for the relevant substantive application.

F9.2 For the avoidance of doubt, this procedure is not normally available in relation to a Case Management Conference or a pre-trial review. Whether or not the parties are agreed as between themselves on the directions that the Court should be asked to consider giving at a Case Management Conference or a pre-trial review, attendance will normally be required. See D8.3.

F9.3 Where an order provides a time by which something is to be done the order should wherever possible state the particular date by

Section F Applications

which the thing is to be done rather than specify a period of time from a particular date or event: rule 2.9.

F.10 Hearing dates, time estimates and time limits

F10.1   Dates for the hearing of applications to be attended by advocates are normally fixed after discussion with the counsel's clerks or with the solicitor concerned.

F10.2   The efficient working of the Court depends on accurate estimates of the time needed for the oral hearing of an application including a considered estimate of the Judge's pre-hearing reading. Over-estimating can be as wasteful as under-estimating.

F10.3   Subject to F10.4, the Commercial Court Listing Office will not ordinarily accept or act on time estimates for the oral hearing of applications where those estimates exceed the following maxima:

Application to challenge jurisdiction/service: 4 hours
Application for summary judgment: 4 hours
Application to set aside/vary interim remedy: 4 hours
Application to set aside default judgment: 2 hours
Application to amend statement of case: 1 hour
Application for specific disclosure: 1 hour
Application for security for costs: 1 hour

F10.4   A longer time length for oral hearing will only be granted upon application in writing specifying the additional time required and giving reasons why it is required. A copy of the written application (which may be by letter, and should be agreed where possible) should be sent to the advocates for all other parties in the case at the same time as it is sent to the Listing Office.

F10.5   **(a)**   Not later than five days before the date fixed for the hearing the applicant must provide the Listing Office with the applicant's current estimate of the time required to dispose of the application.

(b)   If at any time either party considers that there is a material risk that the hearing of the application will exceed the time currently allowed it must inform the Listing Office immediately.

Section F   Applications

F10.6 **(a)** All time estimates should be given on the assumption that the Judge will have read in advance the skeleton arguments and the documents identified in the reading list. In this connection attention is drawn to section F8.

(b) A time estimate for an ordinary application must allow time for judgment and consequential matters; a time estimate for a heavy application should not.

(c) The definition of "heavy application" in F6.1 indicates that an application requiring oral argument of no more than half a day will remain an ordinary application. Therefore the overall time estimate for the hearing of an ordinary application (including judgment and consequential matters) may well be for more than half a day. In order to make it clear that such an application is not a heavy application, the time estimate for an ordinary application must also specify separately the time required for pre-reading, the time required for oral argument, and the time required for judgment and consequential matters

F10.7 Save in the situation referred to at F10.8, a separate estimate must be given for each application, including any application issued after, but to be heard at the same time as, another application.

F10.8 A separate estimate need not be given for any application issued after, but to be heard at the same time as, another application where the advocate in the case certifies in writing that

(a) the determination of the application first issued will necessarily determine the application issued subsequently; or

(b) the matters raised in the application issued subsequently are not contested.

F10.9 If it is found at the hearing that the time required for the hearing has been significantly underestimated, the Judge hearing the application may adjourn the matter and may make any special costs orders (including orders for the immediate payment of costs and wasted costs orders) as may be appropriate.

F10.10 Failure to comply with the requirements for providing bundles for the application will normally result in the application not being heard on the date fixed at the expense of the party in default (see further

Section F Applications

F5.9 and F6.8). An order for immediate payment of costs may be made.

F.11 Application bundles

F11.1 **(a)** Attention is drawn to Appendix 7, which deals with the preparation of bundles (electronic or paper).
(b) Bundles for use on applications may be compiled in any convenient manner but must contain the following documents (preferably in separate sections in the following order):

   (i)   a copy of the application notice;
   (ii) a draft of the order which the applicant seeks;
   (iii) a copy of the statements of case;
   (iv) copies of any previous orders which are relevant to the application;
   (v)   copies of the witness statements and affidavits filed in support of, or in opposition to, the application, together with any exhibits.

(c) Copies of the statements of case and of previous orders in the action should be provided in a separate section of the bundle. They should not be exhibited to witness statements.
(d) Witness statements and affidavits previously filed in the same proceedings should be included in the bundle at a convenient location. They should not be exhibited to witness statements.
(e) Where for the purpose of the application it is likely to be necessary for the Court to read in chronological order correspondence or other documents located as exhibits to different affidavits or witness statements, copies of such documents should be organised and paged in chronological order in a separate composite bundle or bundles which should be agreed between the parties. If time does not permit agreement on the contents of the composite bundle, it is the responsibility of the applicant to prepare the composite bundle and to provide it to the Listing Office by 4pm two clear days (adjusted as provided at F6.4) before the hearing in the case of heavy applications and one clear day before the hearing in the case of all other applications.

Section F Applications

F.12 Chronologies, indices and dramatis personae

F12.1 For most applications it is of assistance for the applicant to provide a chronology which should be cross-referenced to the documents. Dramatis personae are often useful as well.

F12.2 Guidelines on the preparation of chronologies and indices are set out in Appendix 6.

F.13 Authorities

F13.1 On some applications there will be key authorities that it would be useful for the Judge to read before the oral hearing of the application. Copies of these authorities should be provided with the skeleton arguments. In all cases where an authority is cited, the proposition of law demonstrated by the particular authority should be stated and the specific passages in the judgment supporting the proposition should be identified.

F13.2 It is also desirable for bundles of the authorities on which the parties wish to rely to be provided to the Judge hearing the application as soon as possible after skeleton arguments have been exchanged.

F13.3 Authorities should only be cited when they contain some principle of law relevant to an issue arising on the application and where their substance is not to be found in the decision of a Court of higher authority. Practitioners should comply with the 23 March 2012 Practice Note on Citation of Authorities. Specifically, where a judgment is reported in the Official Law Reports that report must be cited. Other series of reports and official transcripts of judgment may only be used when a case is not reported in the Official Law Reports.

F13.4 **(a)** Save exceptionally (e.g. when to do otherwise would involve ending a bundle in mid-case), bundles of authorities that are printed in hard copy should not exceed 300 double-sided pages in length.

(b) Bundles of authorities that are printed in hard copy should (save where there is good reason otherwise, or the Judge otherwise requests) be printed/copied double-sided and be made up as follows:

Section F   Applications

(i) Where the authority is reported, PDF copies or photocopies of the original report with the head-note;
(ii) Where the authority is unreported, the official transcript where available (e.g. the printable RTF version which is available on Bailii).

F.14 Costs

F14.1 The rules governing the award and assessment of costs are contained in CPR Part 44 to 48.

F14.2 Active consideration will generally be given by the Court to adopting the summary assessment procedure in all cases where the schedule of costs of the successful party is no more than £100,000, but the parties should always be prepared for the Court to assess costs summarily even where the costs exceed this amount.

F14.3 In carrying out a summary assessment of costs, the Court may have regard amongst other matters to:

(a) advice from the Chief Costs Judge on costs of specialist solicitors and counsel;
(b) any information published by, or provided to the Court at its request by, one or more of the specialist associations (referred to at A4.2) on average charges by specialist solicitors and counsel.

F14.4 Active consideration will generally be given by the Court to making an order for a payment on account of costs if they are not assessed summarily.

F.15 Interim injunctions

Generally

F15.1 **(a)** Applications for interim injunctions are governed by CPR Part 25.
(b) Applications must be made on notice in accordance with the procedure set out in CPR Part 23 unless there are good reasons for proceeding without notice.

Section F   Applications

F15.2   A party who wishes to make an application for an interim injunction must give the Commercial Court Listing Office as much notice as possible.

F15.3   (a) Except when the application is so urgent that there has not been any opportunity to do so, the applicant must issue a claim form and obtain the evidence on which he wishes to rely in support of the application before making the application.
(b) On applications of any weight, and unless the urgency means that this is not possible, the applicant should provide the Court at the earliest opportunity with a skeleton argument.
(c) An affidavit, and not a witness statement, is required on an application for a freezing order: PD 25A § 3.1.

Fortification of undertakings

F15.4   (a) Where the applicant for an interim remedy is not able to show sufficient assets within the jurisdiction of the Court to provide substance to the undertakings given, particularly the undertaking in damages, it may be required to reinforce the undertakings by providing security.
(b) Security will be ordered in such form as the Judge decides is appropriate but may, for example, take the form of a payment into Court, a bond issued by an insurance company or a first demand guarantee or standby credit issued by a first-class bank.
(c) In an appropriate case the Judge may order a payment to be made to the applicant's solicitors to be held by them as officers of the Court pending further order. Sometimes the undertaking of a parent company may be acceptable.

Form of order

F15.5   A phrase indicating that an interim remedy is to remain in force until judgment or further order means that it remains in force until the delivery of a final judgment. If an interim remedy continuing after judgment is required, say until judgment has been satisfied, an application to that effect must be made (see further section K1).

F15.6   It is good practice to draft an order for an interim remedy so that it includes a proviso which permits acts which would otherwise be

Section F Applications

a breach of the order to be done with the written consent of the solicitor of the other party or parties. This enables the parties to agree in effect to variations (or the discharge) of the order without the necessity of coming back to the Court.

F15.7 Standard forms of wording for freezing injunctions are set out in Appendix 11. The forms of wording have been adapted for use in the Commercial Court. Careful regard should be had to the footnotes included in Appendix 11. The example wording may be modified as appropriate in any particular case. Any modification to the form by an applicant should be expressly referred to the Judge's attention at the application hearing.

Freezing injunctions

F15.8 (a) Freezing injunctions made on an application without notice will provide for a return date, unless the Judge otherwise orders: PD 25 § 5.1(3). In the usual course, the return date given will be a Friday (unless a date for a Case Management Conference has already been fixed, in which event the return date given will in the usual course be that date).

(b) If, after service or notification of the injunction, one or more of the parties considers that more than 30 minutes will be required to deal with the matter on the return date the Listing Office should be informed forthwith and in any event no later than 4 p.m. on the Wednesday before the Friday fixed as the return date.

(c) If the parties agree, the return date may be postponed to a later date on which all parties will be ready to deal with any substantive issues. In this event, an agreed form of order continuing the injunction to the postponed return date should be submitted for consideration by a Judge and if the order is made in the terms submitted there will be no need for the parties to attend on the day originally fixed as the return date. In such a case the defendant and any other interested party will continue to have liberty to apply to vary or set aside the order.

F15.9 A provision for the defendant to give notice of any application to discharge or vary the order is usually included as a matter of

Section F   Applications

convenience but it is not proper to attempt to fetter the right of the defendant to apply without notice or on short notice if need be.

F15.10 As regards freezing orders in respect of assets outside the jurisdiction, the standard wording in relation to effects on third parties should normally incorporate wording to enable overseas branches of banks or similar institutions which have offices within the jurisdiction to comply with what they reasonably believe to be their obligations under the laws of the country where the assets are located or under the proper law of the relevant banking or other contract relating to such assets.

F15.11 Any bank or third party served with, notified of or affected by a freezing injunction may apply to the Court without notice to any party for directions, or notify the Court in writing without notice to any party, in the event that the order affects or may affect the position of the bank or third party under legislation, regulations or procedures aimed to prevent money laundering.

Search orders

F15.12 Search orders are rare. Attention is drawn to the detailed requirements in respect of search orders set out in PD 25A § 7. The applicant for the search order will normally be required to undertake not to inform any third party of the search order or of the case until after a specified date.

Applications to discharge or vary freezing injunctions and search orders

F15.13 Applications to discharge or vary freezing injunctions and search orders are treated as matters of urgency for listing purposes. Those representing applicants for discharge or variation should ascertain before a date is fixed for the hearing whether, having regard to the evidence which they wish to adduce, the claimant would wish to adduce further evidence in opposition. If so, all reasonable steps must be taken by all parties to agree upon the earliest practicable date at which they can be ready for the hearing, so as to avoid the last minute need to vacate a fixed date. In cases of difficulty the matter should be referred to a Judge who may be able to suggest temporary solutions pending the hearing.

F15.14 If a freezing injunction or a search order is discharged on an application to discharge or vary, or on the return date, the Judge will consider whether it is appropriate that he should assess damages at once and direct immediate payment by the applicant. Where the Judge considers that any hearing in connection with the cross undertaking of damages or the assessment of damages should be postponed to a future date she or he will give such case management directions as may be appropriate for the hearing, including, if necessary, disclosure of documents and exchange of witness statements and experts' reports.

Applications under section 25 of the Civil Jurisdiction and Judgments Act 1982

F15.15 A CPR Part 8 claim form (rather than an application notice: cf. rule 25.4(2)) must be used for an application under section 25 of the Civil Jurisdiction and Judgments Act 1982 ("Interim relief in England and Wales and Northern Ireland in the absence of substantive proceedings"). The modified Part 8 procedure used in the Commercial Court is referred to at section B5.

F.16 Security for costs

F16.1 Applications for security for costs are governed by rules 25.12–14.

F16.2 Related practice is set out in Appendix 10.

Section G
Alternative Dispute Resolution ("ADR")

G.1 Generally

G1.1 While emphasising its primary role as a forum for deciding commercial cases, the Commercial Court encourages parties to consider the use of ADR (such as, but not confined to, mediation and conciliation) as an alternative means of resolving disputes or particular issues.

G1.2 Whilst the Commercial Court remains an entirely appropriate forum for resolving most of the disputes which are issued in the Commercial Court, the view of the Commercial Court is that the settlement of disputes by means of ADR:

(a) significantly helps parties to save costs;
(b) saves parties the delay of litigation in reaching finality in their disputes;
(c) enables parties to achieve settlement of their disputes while preserving their existing commercial relationships and market reputation;
(d) provides parties with a wider range of solutions than those offered by litigation; and
(e) is likely to make a substantial contribution to the more efficient use of judicial resources.

G1.3 The Commercial Judges will in appropriate cases invite the parties to consider whether their dispute, or particular issues in it, could be resolved through ADR.

G1.4 Legal representatives in all cases should consider with their clients and the other parties concerned the possibility of attempting to resolve the dispute or particular issues by ADR and should ensure that their clients are fully informed as to the most cost effective means of resolving their dispute.

Section G Alternative Dispute Resolution ("ADR")

G1.5 Parties who consider that ADR might be an appropriate means of resolving the dispute or particular issues in the dispute may apply for directions at any stage, including before service of the defence and before the Case Management Conference.

G1.6 At the Case Management Conference if it should appear to the Judge that the case or any of the issues arising in it are particularly appropriate for an attempt at settlement by means of ADR but that the parties have not previously attempted settlement by such means, she or he may invite the parties to use ADR.

G1.7 The Judge may, if she or he considers it appropriate, adjourn the case for a specified period of time to encourage and enable the parties to use ADR. The Judge may for this purpose extend the time for compliance by the parties or any of them with any requirement under the rules, the Guide or any order of the Court. The Judge in making an order providing for ADR will normally take into account, when considering at what point in the pre-trial timetable there should be compliance with such an order, such matters as the costs likely to be incurred at each stage in the pre-trial timetable if the claim is not settled, the costs of a mediation or other means of dispute resolution, and how far the prospects of a successful mediation or other means of dispute resolution are likely to be enhanced by completion of pleadings, disclosure of documents, provision of further information under CPR Part 18, exchange of factual witness statements or exchange of experts' reports.

G1.8 The Judge may further consider in an appropriate case making an ADR Order in the terms set out in Appendix 3.

G1.9 **(a)** If the parties are unable to agree upon a neutral individual or panel of individuals to act as a mediator, the normal form of ADR order set out in Appendix 3 contains at paragraph 3 a mandatory requirement that the Case Management Conference should be restored to enable the Court to facilitate agreement on a neutral or panel of neutrals. In order to avoid the cost of a restored case management hearing, the parties may agree to send to the Court their respective lists of available neutrals, so as to enable the Judge to suggest a name from those lists.

Section G Alternative Dispute Resolution ("ADR")

- **(b)** In any other case the parties may by consent refer to the Judge for assistance in reaching agreement on a neutral or panel of neutrals.
- **(c)** The Court will not recommend any individual or body to act as a mediator or arbitrator and its assistance at (a) or (b) above is not to be taken as involving recommendation.

G1.10 At the Case Management Conference or at any other hearing in the course of which the Judge makes an order providing for ADR she or he may make such order as to the costs that the parties may incur by reason of their using or attempting to use ADR as may in all the circumstances seem appropriate. The orders for costs are normally either (a) an order for costs in the case, meaning that if the case is not settled, the costs of the ADR procedures will follow the ultimate event, or (b) an order that each side shall bear its own costs of those procedures if the case is not settled.

G1.11 In some cases it may be appropriate that an ADR order should be made following judgment if application is made for permission to appeal. In such cases the Court may adjourn the application for permission to appeal while making an ADR order providing for ADR procedures to be completed within a specified time and, failing settlement with that period, for the application for permission to appeal to be restored.

G1.12 At the Case Management Conference the Court may consider that an order directed to encouraging bilateral negotiations between the parties' respective legal representatives is likely to be a more cost-effective and productive route to settlement then can be offered by a formal ADR Order. In such a case the Court may set a date by which there is to be a meeting between respective solicitors and their respective clients' officials responsible for decision-taking in relation to the case in question.

G.2 Early neutral evaluation

G2.1 Early neutral evaluation ("ENE") is a without-prejudice, non-binding, evaluation of the merits of a dispute or of particular issues in dispute, given after time-limited consideration of core materials and

Section G Alternative Dispute Resolution ("ADR")

having read or listened to concise argument. It is generally designed to take place at an early stage in a dispute, and in private.

G2.2 At a Case Management Conference the Court may explore with the parties, through their advocates, whether early neutral evaluation may assist the parties to resolve their dispute.

G2.3 ENE may be provided by appropriate third parties. However in appropriate cases and with the agreement of all parties the Court will itself provide an ENE. This is one of the Court's powers for the purpose of managing the case and furthering the overriding objective: rule 3.1(2)(m).

G2.4 Where the evaluation is undertaken by a Commercial Judge it will be accompanied only by brief, informal reasons usually expressed orally. The purpose of ENE is to help the parties settle the case: rule 3.1(2)(m).

G2.5 The approval of the Judge in Charge of the Commercial Court must be obtained before any ENE is undertaken by a Commercial Judge.

G2.6 If, after discussion with the advocates representing the parties, it appears to a Judge that an ENE by a Commercial Judge is likely to assist in the resolution of the dispute or of particular issues, she or he will, with the agreement of the parties, refer the matter to the Judge in Charge of the Commercial Court. If the Judge in Charge of the Commercial Court agrees that ENE should be undertaken by a Commercial Judge:

(a) The Judge in Charge of the Commercial Court will nominate a Judge to conduct the ENE.
(b) The Judge who is to conduct the ENE will give such directions for its preparation and conduct as she or he considers appropriate.
(c) The Judge who conducts the ENE will take no further part in the case, either for the purpose of the hearing of applications or as the Judge at trial, unless the parties agree otherwise.

Section H
Evidence for Trial

H.1 Witnesses of fact

Preparation and form of witness statements

H1.1 Witness statements must comply with the requirements of PD 32. The following points are also emphasised:

(a) the function of a witness statement is to set out in writing the evidence in chief of the witness; as far as possible, therefore, the statement should be in the witness's own words;

(b) a witness statement should be as concise as the circumstances of the case allow without omitting any significant matters; there may be no need to deal with (or deal with other than briefly) matters that are common ground;

(c) a witness statement should not contain lengthy quotations from documents;

(d) it is seldom necessary to exhibit documents to a witness statement;

(e) a witness statement should not engage in (legal or other) argument;

(f) a witness statement must indicate which of the statements made in it are made from the witness's own knowledge and which are made on information or belief, giving the source for any statement made on information or belief;

(g) a witness statement must contain a statement by the witness that the witness believes the matters stated in it are true; proceedings for contempt of Court may be brought against a person for making, or causing to be made, a false statement in a witness statement without an honest belief in its truth: rule 32.14(1).

Section H Evidence for Trial

      (h) a witness statement must comply with any direction of the Court about its length. <u>Unless the Court directs otherwise, witness statements should be no more than 30 pages in length.</u>

H1.2 It is usually convenient for a witness statement to follow the chronological sequence of events or matters dealt with (PD 32 § 19.2). It is helpful for it to indicate to which issue in the List of Common Ground and Issues the particular passage in the witness statement relates, either by a heading in the statement or in a marginal notation or by some other convenient method.

H1.3 It is improper to put pressure of any kind on a witness to give anything other than the witness' own account of the matters with which the statement deals. It is also improper to serve a witness statement known to be false or where it is known the maker does not in all respects actually believe the witness statement to be true.

Fluency of witnesses

H1.4 If a witness is not sufficiently fluent in English to give evidence in English, the witness statement should be in the witness' own language and a translation provided.

H1.5 If a witness is not fluent in English but can be understood in broken English and can understand written English, the statement may be in English and need not be in the witness' words provided that these matters are indicated in the statement itself. It must however be written so as to express as accurately as possible the substance of the evidence of the witness.

Witness statement as evidence in chief

H1.6 **(a)** Where a witness is called to give oral evidence, the witness statement of that witness is to stand as the witness' evidence in chief unless the Court orders otherwise: rule 32.5(2).

      (b) In an appropriate case the trial Judge may direct that the whole or any part of a witness's evidence in chief is to be given orally. This course may be taken on the Judge's own initiative or on application by a party. Notice of an application for such an

Section H   Evidence for Trial

order should be given as early as is reasonably convenient. It is usually reasonable for any such application to be made at a pre-trial review if one is held.

Additional evidence from a witness

H1.7 (a) A witness giving oral evidence at trial may with the permission of the Court amplify the witness statement and give evidence in relation to new matters which have arisen since the witness statement was served: rule 32.5(3). Permission will be given only if the Court considers that there is good reason not to confine the evidence of the witness to the contents of the witness statement: rule 32.5(4). The matter should be discussed between advocates for each party before the witness is called.

(b) A supplemental witness statement should normally be served where the witness proposes materially to add to, alter, correct or retract from what is in the original statement. Permission will be required for the service of a supplemental statement. Such application should be made at the pre-trial review or, if there is no pre-trial review, as early as possible before the start of the trial. If application is made at any later stage, the applicant must provide compelling evidence explaining its delay in adducing such evidence.

(c) It is the duty of all parties to ensure that the statements of all factual witnesses intended to be called or whose statements are to be tendered as hearsay statements should be exchanged simultaneously unless the Court has otherwise ordered. Witnesses additional to those whose statements have been initially exchanged may only be called with the permission of the Court which will not normally be given unless prompt application is made supported by compelling evidence explaining the late introduction of that witness' evidence.

Notice of decision not to call a witness

H1.8 (a) If a party decides not to call to give oral evidence at trial a witness whose statement has been served but wishes to rely upon the evidence, the party must put in the statement as hearsay

Section H   Evidence for Trial

evidence unless the Court otherwise orders: rule 32.5. If the party proposes to put the evidence in as hearsay evidence, reference should be made to CPR Part 33.

(b) If the party who has served the statement does not put it in as hearsay evidence, any other party may do so: rule 32.5(5).

Witness summonses

H1.9 (a) CPR Part 34 deals with witness summonses, including a summons for a witness to attend Court or to produce documents in advance of the date fixed for trial.

(b) Witness summonses are served by the parties, not the Court.

H.2   Expert witnesses

Application for permission to call an expert witness

H2.1 Any application for permission to call an expert witness or serve an expert's report should normally be made at the Case Management Conference.

H2.2 The party applying for such permission will be expected to provide an estimate of the costs of the proposed expert evidence.

H2.3 The party applying for permission to call an expert witness will be expected to identify to which issue or issues in the List of Common Ground and Issues the proposed expert evidence relates, and to propose any amendments to the List of Common Ground and Issues that might be required for this purpose.

H2.4 The Court may specify in any order it makes the issues which the expert should address and may limit the length of an expert report.

H2.5 If a witness is not sufficiently fluent in English to give evidence in English, the expert report should be in the witness's own language and a translation provided.

H2.6 Expert evidence can lead to unnecessary expense and the parties should be prepared to consider the use of single joint experts in appropriate cases. In many cases the use of single joint experts is not appropriate and each party will generally be given permission

Section H   Evidence for Trial

to call one expert in each field requiring expert evidence. These are referred to in the Guide as "separate experts".

H2.7 When the use of a single joint expert is contemplated, and in many cases where separate experts are to be used, the Court will expect the parties to co-operate in developing, and agreeing to the greatest possible extent, terms of reference for the expert(s).

H2.8 In most cases the terms of reference will (in particular) identify in detail what the expert is asked to do, identify any documentary materials the expert is asked to consider and specify any assumptions she or he is asked to make.

Provisions of general application in relation to expert evidence

H2.9 The provisions set out in Appendix 8 to the Guide apply to all aspects of expert evidence (including expert reports, meetings of experts and expert evidence given orally) unless the Court orders otherwise. Parties should ensure that they are drawn to the attention of any experts they instruct at the earliest opportunity.

Form and content of expert's reports

H2.10 The Court will restrict expert evidence to that which is reasonably required to resolve the proceedings: rule 35.1. The Court will consider whether expert evidence is necessary at all, and, where it is necessary, how it may make the best contribution and how its length and cost may best be controlled.

H2.11 Expert's reports must comply with the requirements of PD 35. The following particular points are emphasised:

(a) In stating the substance of all material instructions (written or oral) on the basis of which her or his report is written as required by rule 35.10(3) and PD 35 § 3.2(3) an expert witness should state (i) the facts and (ii) the assumptions upon which her or his opinion is based.

(b) The expert must make it clear which, if any, of the facts stated are within the expert's own direct knowledge.

(c) If a stated assumption is, in the opinion of the expert witness, unreasonable or unlikely she or he should state that clearly.

Section H Evidence for Trial

- **(d)** The expert's report must be limited to matters relevant to the issue or issues in the List of Common Ground and Issues to which the relevant expert evidence relates and for which permission to call such expert evidence has been given.
- **(e)** The report of an expert should be as concise as possible.

H2.12 It is useful if a report contains a glossary of significant technical terms.

H2.13 Where the evidence of an expert, such as a surveyor, assessor, adjuster, or other investigator is to be relied upon for the purpose of establishing primary facts, such as the condition of a ship or other property as found by the expert at a particular time, as well as for the purpose of deploying her or his expertise to express an opinion on any matter related to or in connection with the primary facts, that part of her or his evidence which is to be relied upon to establish the primary facts, is to be treated as factual evidence to be incorporated into a factual witness statement to be exchanged in accordance with the order for the exchange of factual witness statements. The purpose of this practice is to avoid postponing disclosure of a party's factual evidence until service of expert reports.

Statement of truth

H2.14
- **(a)** The report must be signed by the expert and must contain a statement of truth in accordance with CPR Part 35.
- **(b)** Proceedings for contempt of Court may be brought against a person if he makes, or causes to be made, without an honest belief in its truth, a false statement in an expert's report verified in the manner set out in this section.

Request by an expert to the Court for directions

H2.15 An expert may provide to the Court a written request for directions to assist in carrying out the function of expert, but

- **(a)** at least 7 days before the expert does so (or such shorter period as the Court may direct) the expert should provide a copy of the proposed request to the party instructing her or him; and
- **(b)** at least 4 days before the expert provides the request to the Court (or such shorter period as the Court may direct) the

Section H   Evidence for Trial

expert should provide a copy of the proposed request to all other parties.

Exchange of reports

H2.16 In appropriate cases the Court will direct that the reports of expert witnesses be exchanged sequentially rather than simultaneously.

H2.17 The sequential exchange of expert reports may in many cases save time and costs by helping to focus the contents of responsive reports upon actual rather than assumed issues of expert evidence and by avoiding repetition of detailed factual material as to which there is no real issue.

H2.18 Among the areas of expert evidence where sequential exchange is likely to be particularly effective are where experts are giving evidence of foreign law or are forensic accountants. This is an issue that the Court will normally wish to consider at the Case Management Conference.

Meetings of expert witnesses

H2.19 The Court will normally direct a meeting or meetings of expert witnesses before trial.

H2.20 Consideration should be given to whether experts should meet before they prepare their expert reports.

H2.21 Sometimes it may be useful for there to be further meetings during the trial itself.

H2.22 The purposes of a meeting of experts are to give the experts the opportunity:

(a) to discuss the expert issues;
(b) to decide, with the benefit of that discussion, on which expert issues they share or can come to share the same expert opinion and on which expert issues there remains a difference of expert opinion between them (and what that difference is).

H2.23 Subject to H2.25, the content of the discussion between the experts at or in connection with a meeting is without prejudice and shall not be referred to at the trial unless the parties so agree: rule 35.12(4).

Section H Evidence for Trial

H2.24 Subject to any directions of the Court, the procedure to be adopted at a meeting of experts is a matter for the experts themselves, not the parties or their legal representatives.

H2.25 Neither the parties nor their legal representatives should seek to restrict the freedom of experts to identify and acknowledge the expert issues on which they agree at, or following further consideration after, meetings of experts.

H2.26 Unless the Court orders otherwise, at or following any meeting the experts should prepare a joint memorandum for the Court recording

   (a) the fact that they have met and discussed the expert issues;
   (b) the issues on which they agree;
   (c) the issues on which they disagree; and
   (d) a brief summary of the reasons for their disagreement.

H2.27 If experts reach agreement on an issue that agreement shall not bind the parties unless the parties expressly agree to be bound by it.

Written questions to experts

H2.28 **(a)** Under rule 35.6 a party may, without the permission of the Court, put proportionate written questions to an expert instructed by another party (or to a single joint expert) about that expert's report. Unless the Court gives permission or the other party agrees, such questions must be for the purpose only of clarifying the report.

   (b) The Court will pay close attention to the use of this procedure (especially where separate experts are instructed) to ensure that it remains an instrument for the helpful exchange of information. The Court will not allow it to interfere with the procedure for an exchange of professional opinion at a meeting of experts, or to inhibit that exchange of professional opinion. In cases where (for example) questions that are oppressive in number or content are put, or questions are put for any purpose other than clarification of the report, the Court will not hesitate to disallow the questions and to make an appropriate order for costs against the party putting them.

Section H   Evidence for Trial

Documents referred to in experts' reports

H2.29 Unless they have already been provided on inspection of documents at the stage of disclosure, copies of any photographs, plans, analyses, measurements, survey reports or other similar documents relied on by an expert witness as well as copies of any unpublished sources must be provided to all parties at the same time as the report.

H2.30 **(a)** Rule 31.14(2) provides that (subject to rule 35.10(4)) a party may inspect a document mentioned in an expert's report. In a commercial case an expert's report will frequently, and helpfully, list all or many of the relevant previous documents (published or unpublished) or books written by the expert or to which the expert has contributed. Requiring inspection of this material may often be unrealistic, and the collating and copying burden could be huge.

(b) Accordingly, a party wishing to inspect a document in an expert report that does not fall within H2.29 (which documents are to be provided as there specified) should (failing agreement) make an application to the Court. The Court will not permit inspection unless it is satisfied that it is necessary for the just disposal of the case and that the document is not reasonably available to the party making the application from an alternative source.

Trial

H2.31 In cases where the expert evidence is complex and where issues may fall away during exchange of reports and/or expert meetings the Court will consider at the Case Management Conference with the parties a direction that the trial reading list for the Judge:

(a) identify the issues that the Court will be asked to decide with the assistance of expert evidence;

(b) in respect of each such issue, briefly state each party's case;

(c) in respect of each such issue, identify the pages of the expert evidence that need in the opinion of the trial advocates to be read.

H2.32 At trial the evidence of expert witnesses is usually taken as a block, after the evidence of witnesses of fact has been given.

H2.33 The introduction of additional expert evidence after the commencement of the trial can have a severely disruptive effect. Not only is it likely to make necessary additional expert evidence in response, but it may also lead to applications for further disclosure of documents and also to applications to call further factual evidence from witnesses whose statements have not previously been exchanged. Accordingly, experts' supplementary reports must be completed and exchanged by the date ordered for such reports and, where no date is ordered, not later than the progress monitoring date. The introduction of additional expert evidence after the relevant date will only be permitted upon application to the trial Judge and if there are very strong grounds for admitting it.

H2.34 The Court may direct that some or all of the experts from like disciplines shall give their evidence concurrently: PD 35 § 11.1. The Court may require this of its own initiative, or the parties may propose it. The matter should be discussed between advocates. The Court may modify the procedure at PD 35 § 11 and will consider whether itself to initiate the questioning of the experts or to invite the parties' representatives to do so.

H.3 Evidence by video link

H3.1 In an appropriate case permission may be given for the evidence of a witness to be given by video link. If permission is given the Court will give directions for the conduct of this part of the trial.

H3.2 The party seeking permission to call evidence by video link should prepare and serve on all parties and provide to the Court a memorandum dealing with the matters outlined in the Video Conferencing Guidance contained in Annex 3 to PD 32 and setting out precisely what arrangements are proposed. Where the proposal involves transmission from a location with no existing video-link facility, experience shows that questions of feasibility, timing and cost will require particularly close investigation.

H3.3 An application for permission to call evidence by video link should be made, if possible, at the Case Management Conference or, at the latest, at any pre-trial review. However, an application may be made at

Section H   Evidence for Trial

an even later stage if necessary. Particular attention should be given to the taking of evidence by video link whenever a proposed witness will have to travel from a substantial distance abroad and evidence is likely to last no more than half a day.

H3.4 In considering whether to give permission for evidence to be given in this way the Court will be concerned in particular to balance any potential savings of costs against the inability to observe the witness at first hand when giving evidence.

H.4   Taking evidence abroad

H4.1 The Court is well used to video link to provide evidence from a witness who is abroad: see section H3.

H4.2 In an appropriate case permission may be given for the evidence of a witness to be taken abroad. CPR Part 34 contains provisions for the taking of evidence by deposition, and the issue of letters of request.

H4.3 In a very exceptional case, and subject in particular to all necessary approvals being obtained and diplomatic requirements being satisfied, the Court may be willing to conduct part of the proceedings abroad. The Court is unlikely to take that course if there is any reasonable opportunity for a witness to give evidence by video link.

Section J
Trial

J.1 Expedited trial; Shorter Trials Scheme; Flexible Trials Scheme

J1.1 The Commercial Court is able to provide an expedited trial in cases of sufficient urgency and importance.

J1.2 A party seeking an expedited trial should apply to the Judge in Charge of the Commercial Court on notice to all parties at the earliest possible opportunity. The application should normally be made after issue and service of the claim form but before service of particulars of claim.

J1.3 As provided at D2.2, the parties should consider, ordinarily before proceedings commence or at least in advance of the first Case Management Conference, whether a case is suitable for the Shorter Trials Scheme or the Flexible Trials Scheme in the interest of reducing the length and cost of trial: PD 51N. For example the parties may be able to agree (subject to the Court) to confine matters (including the time allowed to each party at trial) so that a case which might ordinarily take longer at trial can be tried in a shorter period under the Shorter Trials Scheme.

J.2 Trials of issues

J2.1 The Court may direct a separate trial of any issue under rule 3.1(2)(i). It will sometimes be advantageous to have a separate trial of particular issues with other issues being heard either by the same Judge or by another Commercial Judge or in another Court or tribunal. For example, where liability is tried first in the Commercial Court, the parties may choose to ask an arbitrator to decide questions of damages. The same approach can be applied to other factual

Section J Trial

questions once the Court has decided issues of principle or of general application.

J2.2 Under rule 3.1(2)(j), (k) and (l) the Court may decide the order in which issues are to be tried, may exclude an issue from consideration and may dismiss or give judgment on a claim after a decision on a preliminary issue. The Court is likely to consider this by reference to the List of Common Ground and Issues. Particularly in long trials, it will sometimes be advantageous to exercise these powers, and accordingly hear the evidence relevant to some issues before moving on to the evidence relevant to others; and the Judge will sometimes decide some issues before moving on to hear the evidence relevant to other issues.

J.3 Information technology at trial, including paperless trials

J3.1 The use of IT at trial is strongly encouraged where it is likely to save time and cost or to increase accuracy. Paperless trials in particular are strongly encouraged, except where the cost would be too great for a party (in this connection, see further J3.4).

J3.2 If any party considers that it would be advantageous to make use of IT in preparation for, or at, trial, the matter should be raised at the first Case Management Conference. This is particularly important if it is considered that document handling systems would assist disclosure and inspection of documents or the use of documents at trial. In any event, at the first Case Management Conference or subsequently, even if neither party itself raises the use of IT, the parties must expect the Court to consider its use, including its use at trial.

J3.3 Where IT is to be used for the purposes of presenting the case at trial the same system must be used by all parties and must be made available to the Court.

J3.4 In deciding whether and to what extent IT should be used at the trial the Court will have regard to the financial resources of the parties and where those resources are unequal it will consider whether it is appropriate that, having regard to the parties' unequal financial resources, the party applying for the use of such IT should initially bear the cost subject to the Court's ultimate orders as to the overall costs of the case following judgment.

J.4 Documents for trial

J4.1 The parties should discuss the use of electronic copy or hard copy documents at trial, or a combination.

J4.2 Bundles of documents (electronic or paper) for the trial must be prepared in accordance with Appendix 7.

J4.3 The number, content and organisation of the trial bundles must be approved by the advocates with the conduct of the trial.

J4.4 Apart from certain specified documents, trial bundles should include only necessary documents: PD 39A § 3.2(11). Consideration must always be given to what documents are and are not necessary. Where the Court is of the opinion that costs have been wasted by the inclusion or copying of unnecessary documents it will have no hesitation in making a special order for costs against the person responsible.

J4.5 The number content and organisation of the trial bundles should be agreed in accordance with the following procedure, unless otherwise directed:

(a) the claimant must submit proposals to all other parties at least 6 weeks before the date fixed for trial; and

(b) the other parties must submit details of additions they require and any suggestions for revision of the claimant's proposals to the claimant at least 4 weeks before the date fixed for trial.

All information in this procedure must be supplied in a form that will be most convenient for the recipient to understand, use and respond to. The form to be used should be discussed between the parties before the information is supplied.

J4.6 **(a)** It is the responsibility of the claimant's legal representative to prepare and provide the agreed trial bundles: see PD 39A § 3.4.

(b) If another party wishes to put before the Court a bundle that the claimant regards as unnecessary the other party must prepare and provide it.

J4.7 (a) Preparation of the trial bundles must be completed not later than 10 days before the date for service of skeleton arguments under section J6 unless the Court orders otherwise.

(b) Any party preparing a trial bundle should, as a matter of course, provide all other parties who are to take part in the trial with a copy (see PD 39A § 3.10), at the cost of the receiving party. Further copies should be supplied on request, again at the cost of the receiving party.

J4.8 Unless the Court orders otherwise, a full set of the trial bundles must be provided with the Listing Office two clear days before the start of the designated reading period (see J6.2) and in any event at least 7 days before the date fixed for trial. The core bundle should be prepared and provided at the latest by the time of providing the first trial skeleton argument.

J4.9 If bundles are provided late, this may result in the trial not commencing on the date fixed, at the expense of the party in default. An order for immediate payment of costs may be made.

J4.10 If oral evidence is to be given at trial, the claimant should provide a clean unmarked set of all relevant trial bundles for use in the witness box: PD 39A § 3.10. The claimant is responsible for ensuring that these bundles are kept up to date throughout the trial.

J.5 Reading lists, authorities and trial timetable

J5.1 Unless the Court orders otherwise, a single reading list approved by all advocates must be provided to the Listing Office not later than the time at which the Claimant's skeleton argument is provided under section J6. A reading list should be organised to assist the Judge in preparing efficiently and time-effectively for the trial. Where possible the list should identify the particular sections, pages or paragraphs of a document that in the opinion of the trial advocates need to be read. In a complex case the list might be organised by issue if the trial advocates consider that will assist the Judge.

J5.2 (a) If any party objects to the Judge reading any witness statement or document in advance of the trial, the objection and its grounds should be clearly stated in a letter accompanying the trial bundles and in the skeleton argument of that party.

Section J   Trial

- **(b)** In the absence of objection, the Judge will be free to read the witness statements and documents in advance.
- **(c)** The parties may agree that the Judge should read a witness statement or document in advance on the basis that argument objecting to the witness statement or document will be heard in due course and if the objection is upheld the Judge will reach her or his decisions in the case without taking the witness statement or document into account.

J5.3
- **(a)** A composite bundle of the authorities referred to in the skeleton arguments should be provided to the Listing Office as soon as possible after skeleton arguments have been exchanged.
- **(b)** Unless otherwise agreed, the preparation of the bundle of authorities is the responsibility of the claimant, who should provide copies to all other parties. Advocates should liaise in relation to the production of bundles of authorities to ensure that the same authority does not appear in more than one bundle.

J5.4 Cases which are unreported should normally only be cited where the advocate is ready to give an assurance that the transcript contains a statement of some relevant principle of law of which the substance, as distinct from some mere choice of phraseology, is not to be found in any judgment that has appeared in one of the general or specialised series of law reports.

J5.5
- **(a)** When providing the reading list the claimant should also provide a trial timetable.
- **(b)** A trial timetable may have been fixed by the Judge at the pre-trial review (D18.4). If it has not, the trial timetable should be prepared by the advocate(s) for the claimant after consultation with the advocate(s) for all other parties.
- **(c)** If there are differences of view between the advocate(s) for the claimant and the advocate(s) for other parties, these should be shown.
- **(d)** The trial timetable will provide for oral submissions, witness evidence and expert evidence over the course of the trial. It should also usually provide for written closing submissions. On the first day of the trial the Judge may fix the trial timetable, subject to any further order.

Section J Trial

(e) The parties must comply with the trial timetable. The Court may restrict evidence or submissions to ensure compliance with the trial timetable.

J.6 Skeleton arguments etc. at trial

J6.1 Written skeleton arguments should be prepared by each party. Guidelines on the preparation of skeleton arguments are set out in Appendix 5.

J6.2 Unless otherwise ordered, the skeleton arguments should be served on all other parties and provided to the Court as follows

(a) by the claimant, not later than 1 p.m. two days (i.e. two clear days) before the Judge's reading period for the trial commences or (if no reading period has been directed) two days (i.e. two clear days) before the start of the trial; save that, if this would result in service and provision on a Friday, then the skeleton arguments should be served and provided not later than 1pm on the Thursday;

(b) by each of the defendants, not later than 1 p.m. the day after the day on which the applicant's skeleton argument is required to be served and provided.

J6.3 Advocates are reminded that the timetable and the requisite reading time should be discussed between the advocates, that a careful estimate should be given at the time of the pre-trial checklist/review and any change in the estimates for trial or reading time should be promptly notified to the Commercial Court Office.

J6.4 The claimant should provide a chronology with its skeleton argument. Indices (i.e. documents that collate key references on particular points, or a substantive list of the contents of a particular bundle or bundles) and dramatis personae should also be provided where these are likely to be useful. Guidelines on the preparation of chronologies and indices are set out in Appendix 6. They should be agreed where possible.

J6.5 So far as possible trial skeleton arguments should be limited in length to 50 pages (font minimum 12 point; 1.5 line spacing). Where the advocate or advocates for trial consider that it is not possible to comply with that limit, the matter should be discussed with the trial Judge at the pre-trial review or in correspondence. The provisions

Section J Trial

as to the length of skeleton arguments reflect the experience of the Commercial Judges over time as to what is most useful to the Court.

J.7 Trial sitting days and hearing trials in public

J7.1 Trial sitting days will not normally include Fridays.

J7.2 Where it is necessary in order to accommodate hearing evidence from certain witnesses or types of witness, the Court may agree to sit outside normal hours.

J7.3 The general rule is that a hearing is to be in public: rule 39.2(1).

J7.4 Save in exceptional circumstances, even the most substantial and complex trial should not exceed 12 weeks in length. The parties should work together, and with the Court, to limit the argument and evidence and organise the trial timetable so as to fit the trial within this limit.

J.8 Oral opening statements at trial

J8.1 Oral opening statements should as far as possible be uncontroversial and in any event no longer than the circumstances require. Even in a very heavy case, oral opening statements may be very short.

J8.2 At the conclusion of the opening statement for the claimant the advocates for each of the other parties will usually each be invited to make a short opening statement.

J8.3 It may be convenient to allow a gap between opening statements and the commencement of the evidence at trial.

J8.4 Where a trial is to be listed with a length of 8 weeks or more, consideration may be given to the question whether the opening statements should take place before the end of the previous legal term.

J8.5 When agreeing bundles for trial, legal representatives should bear in mind the effect of the Civil Evidence Act 1995 and of rules 32.19 (notice requiring proof of authenticity) and 33.2(3) (hearsay notices). Pursuant to those provisions, documents which have not been the subject of a notice served in accordance with rule 32.19(2) (requiring proof of authenticity) will be admissible as evidence of the truth of their contents even if there has been noncompliance with the notice requirements of s. 2(1) of the 1995 Act and rule 33.2 (see s.2(4) of the Act). Accordingly, save for documents in respect of which there has been a timely notice to prove authenticity, all documents in the trial bundle will be admissible in evidence without more.

J8.6 However the fact that documents in the trial bundle are admissible in evidence does not mean that all such documents have been adduced in evidence so as to form part of the evidence in the trial. For this to happen either the parties must agree that the document in question is to be treated as put in evidence by one or other of them and the Judge so informed or they must actively adduce the document in evidence by some other means. This might be done by the advocate inviting the Judge to read the document relied upon before the calling of oral evidence. This should be done in the written opening statement or in the oral opening statement if the document is then available. The appropriate procedure will be a matter requiring the exercise of judgment by the advocates in each case.

J8.7 Ultimately it is the trial advocate's responsibility to indicate clearly to the Court before closing her or his case the written evidence which forms part of that case. Whichever course is adopted, it will not normally be appropriate for reliance to be placed in final speeches on any document, not already specifically adduced in evidence by one of the means described.

J.9 Applications in the course of trial

J9.1 It will not normally be necessary for an application notice to be issued for an application which is to be made during the course of the trial, but all other parties should be given adequate notice of the intention to apply.

J9.2 Unless the Judge directs otherwise the parties should prepare skeleton arguments for the hearing of the application.

J.10 Oral closing submissions at trial

J10.1 All parties will be expected to make oral closing submissions, whether or not closing submissions have been made in writing. It is a matter

Section J Trial

for the advocate to consider how in all the circumstances these oral submissions should be presented.

J10.2 Unless the trial Judge directs otherwise, the claimant will make oral closing submissions first, followed by the defendant(s) in the order in which they appear on the claim form, with the claimant having a right of reply.

J.11 Written closing submissions at trial

J11.1 (a) The Court will normally also require closing submissions in writing before oral closing submissions.
(b) Generally advocates should be ready to discuss with the Court, in advance of preparation, the form of and the length of written closing submissions.

J.12 Judgment

J12.1 (a) When judgment is reserved the Judge may deliver judgment orally or by handing down a written judgment. If the Judge delivers judgment orally and a transcript of the judgment is required, a draft of the transcript will initially be provided directly by the transcribers to the Judge (and to the Judge only) for approval. It is the responsibility of the parties to make available to the transcribers any copies of documents or authorities that they require to complete the transcript. The parties may also be asked by the transcribers to check the accuracy of quotations before the draft of the transcript is provided to the Judge for approval, and for this purpose the relevant extracts only (and not the draft transcript as a whole) may be made available by the transcribers to the parties.
(b) If the Judge intends to hand down a written judgment a copy of the draft text marked "Draft Judgment" and bearing the rubric:

"This is a judgment to which the Practice Direction supplementing CPR Part 40 applies. It will be handed down on [] at [] in Court No []. This draft is confidential to the parties and their legal representatives and accordingly neither the draft itself nor its substance may be disclosed to any other person or used in the public domain. The parties must take all reasonable steps to ensure that

Section J Trial

its confidentiality is preserved. No action is to be taken (other than internally) in response to the draft before judgment has been formally pronounced. A breach of any of these obligations may be treated as a contempt of Court. The official version of the judgment will be available from the Courts Recording and Transcription Unit of the Royal Courts of Justice once it has been approved by the Judge.

The Court is likely to wish to hand down its judgment in an approved final form. The advocate should therefore submit any list of typing corrections and other obvious errors of a similar nature in writing (Nil returns are required) to the clerk to [], by email at [], by [] on [], so that changes can be incorporated, if the Judge accepts them, in the handed down judgment."

will normally be supplied to the advocates before the judgment is to be delivered.

- (c) Advocates should inform the Judge's Clerk within the time specified or (where no time is specified) not later than noon on the day before judgment is to be handed down of any typographical or other obvious errors of a similar nature which the Judge might wish to correct. This facility is confined to the correction of textual mistakes and is not to be used as the occasion for attempting to persuade the Judge to change the decision on matters of substance.
- (d) The requirement to treat the text as confidential must be strictly observed. Failure to do so amounts to a contempt of Court.

J12.2 (a) Judgment is not delivered until it is formally pronounced in open Court.
 (b) When the judgment is formally pronounced in open Court, copies of the approved judgment will be made available to the parties, to law reporters and to any other person wanting a copy.
 (c) The Judge may direct that the written judgment stand as the definitive record and that no transcript need be made. Any editorial corrections made at the time of handing down will be incorporated in an approved official text as soon as possible,

and the approved official text, so marked, will be available from the Mechanical Recording Department.

J12.3 If at the time of pronouncement of the judgment any party wishes to apply for permission to appeal to the Court of Appeal, that application should be supported by written draft grounds of appeal.

J12.4 Orders on Judgment should be drawn up in accordance with, and contain the information referred to in D19.1(c).

J.13 Costs

J13.1 The rules governing the award and assessment of costs are contained in CPR Parts 44 to 47.

J13.2 The summary assessment procedure provided for in CPR Part 44 and PD 44 also applies to trials lasting one day or less.

J.14 Interest

J14.1 Historically the Commercial Court generally awarded interest at base rate plus one percent unless that was shown to be unfair to one party or the other or to be otherwise inappropriate. There is now no longer a presumption that base rate plus one percent is the appropriate measure of a commercial rate of interest.

Section K
After Trial

K.1 Continuation, variation and discharge of interim remedies and undertakings

K1.1 **(a)** Applications to continue, vary or discharge interim remedies or undertakings should be made to a Commercial Judge, even after trial.

(b) If a party wishes to continue a freezing injunction after trial or judgment, care should be taken to ensure that the application is made before the existing freezing injunction has expired.

K.2 Accounts and enquiries

K2.1 The Court may order that accounts and inquiries be referred to the Judge of another Court. Alternatively, the parties may choose to refer the matter to arbitration.

K.3 Enforcement

K3.1 Unless the Court orders otherwise, and save for matters in the Financial List, all proceedings for the enforcement of any judgment or order for the payment of money given or made in the Commercial Court will be referred automatically to a Master of the Queen's Bench Division or a District Judge: PD 58 § 1.2(2).

K3.2 In particular cases, for example a case involving questions of enforcement of sovereign debt, particular consideration should be given to a Commercial Judge retaining conduct of the proceedings rather than enforcement being referred automatically to master or a District Judge.

Section K   After Trial

K3.3 Applications in connection with the enforcement of a judgment or order for the payment of money should otherwise be directed to the Registry which will allocate them to the Admiralty Registrar or to one of the Queen's Bench Masters as appropriate.

K.4 Assessment of damages or interest after a default judgment

K4.1 Unless the Court orders otherwise, the assessment of damages or interest following the entry of a default judgment for damages or interest to be assessed will be carried out by the Admiralty Registrar or one of the Queen's Bench Masters to whom the case is allocated by the Registry.

Section L
Multi-party Disputes

L.1 Early consideration

L1.1 Cases which involve, or are expected to involve, a large number of claimants or defendants require close case management from the earliest point. The same is true where there are, or are likely to be, a large number of separate cases involving the same or similar issues. Both classes of case are referred to as "multi-party" disputes.

L1.2 **(a)** The Judge in Charge of the Commercial Court should be informed as soon as it becomes apparent that a multi-party dispute exists or is likely to exist and an early application for directions should be made.

(b) In an appropriate case an application for directions may be made before issue of a claim form. In some cases it may be appropriate for an application to be made without notice in the first instance.

L.2 Available procedures

L2.1 In some cases it may be appropriate for the Court to make a Group Litigation Order under CPR Part 19 and PD 19B. In other cases it may be more convenient for the Court to exercise its general powers of management. These include powers

(a) to dispense with statements of case;
(b) to direct parties to serve outline statements of case;
(c) to direct that cases be consolidated or managed and tried together;
(d) to direct that certain cases or issues be determined before others and to stay other proceedings in the meantime;

Section L Multi-party Disputes

(e) to advance or put back the usual time for pre-trial steps to be taken (for example the disclosure of documents by one or more parties or a payment into Court).

L2.2 Attention is drawn to the provisions of Section III of CPR Part 19, rules 19.10–19.15 and PD 19B. Practitioners should note that the provisions of Section III of CPR Part 19 give the Court additional powers to manage disputes involving multiple claimants or defendants. They should also note that a Group Litigation Order in the Commercial Court (as part of the Queen's Bench Division) may not be made without the consent of the President of the Queen's Bench Division: PD 19B § 3.3(1).

L2.3 An application for a Group Litigation Order should be made in the first instance to the Judge in Charge of the Commercial Court: PD 19B § 3.5.

Section M
Litigants in Person

M.1 The litigant in person

M1.1 Litigants in person (parties representing themselves and without separate legal representation) appear less often in the Commercial Court than in some other Courts. Notwithstanding, their position requires special consideration.

M1.2 Litigants in person are not required to file or provide documents electronically. Enquiry should be made of the Listing Office for convenient alternative arrangements for filing or providing documents.

M1.3 When at least one party is unrepresented the Court, in exercising its powers of case management, will have regard to that fact: rule 3.1A(2). It will adopt at any hearing such procedure as it considers appropriate to further the overriding objective of dealing with the case justly and at proportionate cost: rule 3.1A(4). In relation to taking evidence see also rule 3.1A(5).

M1.4 The Court may encourage an unrepresented party to seek pro bono or other assistance.

M1.5 The Bar Council of England and Wales publishes online a free of charge "Guide to Representing Yourself in Court". The RCJ Advice Bureau publishes a series of free of charge "Going to Court" Guides available online through the Advicenow websit (www.advicenow.org.uk)

M.2 Represented parties

M2.1 Where a litigant in person is involved in a case the Court will expect solicitors and counsel for other parties to do what they reasonably can to ensure that the litigant in person has a fair opportunity to prepare and put her or his case. The Court will expect solicitors and counsel for other parties to have regard to the "Litigants in Person: Guidelines for Lawyers" published jointly by the Bar Council, the Law Society and the Chartered Institute of Legal Executives in June 2015.

M2.2 The duty of an advocate to ensure that the Court is informed of all relevant decisions and legislative provisions of which she or he is aware (whether favourable to the case of her or his client or not) and to bring any procedural irregularity to the attention of the Court during the hearing is of particular importance in a case where a litigant in person is involved.

M2.3 Further, the Court will expect solicitors and counsel appearing for other parties to ensure that the case memorandum, the List of Common Ground and Issues and all necessary bundles are prepared and provided to the Court in accordance with the Guide, even where the litigant in person is unwilling or unable to participate.

M2.4 If the claimant is a litigant in person the Judge at the Case Management Conference will normally direct which of the parties is to have responsibility for the preparation and upkeep of the case management bundle.

M2.5 At the Case Management Conference the Court may give directions relating to the costs of providing application bundles, trial bundles and, if applicable, transcripts of hearings to the litigant in person.

M.3 Companies without representation

M3.1 Although rule 39.6 allows a company or other corporation with the permission of the Court to be represented at trial by an employee, the complexity of most cases in the Commercial Court makes that unsuitable (cf. PD 39A § 5.3). Accordingly, permission is likely to be given only in unusual circumstances.

Section N
Admiralty

N.1 General

N1.1 Proceedings in the Admiralty Court are dealt with in CPR Part 61 and its associated practice direction.

N1.2 The Commercial Court Guide has been prepared in consultation with the Admiralty Judge. It has been adopted to provide guidance about the conduct of proceedings in the Admiralty Court. The Guide must be followed in the Admiralty Court unless the content of CPR Part 61, its associated practice direction or the terms of this section N require otherwise.

N1.3 One significant area of difference between practice in the Commercial Court and practice in the Admiralty Court is that many interlocutory applications are heard by the Admiralty Registrar who has all the powers of the Admiralty Judge save as provided otherwise: rule 61.1(4).

N.2 The Admiralty Court Committee

N2.1 The Admiralty Court Committee provides a specific forum for contact and consultation between the Admiralty Court and its users. Its meetings are usually held in conjunction with the Commercial Court Users Committee. Any correspondence should be addressed to the Deputy Admiralty Marshal, 7 Rolls Building, Fetter Lane, London, EC4A 1NL.

N.3 Commencement of proceedings, service of Statements of Case and associated matters

N3.1 Sections B and C of this guide apply to all Admiralty claims except:

Section N Admiralty

(a) a claim in rem;
(b) a collision claim; and
(c) a limitation claim.

N.4 Commencement and early stages of a claim in rem

N4.1 The early stages of an in rem claim differ from those of other claims. The procedure is governed generally by rule 61.3 and PD 61 § § 3.1–3.11.

N4.2 In addition, the following provisions of the Guide apply to claims in rem: B4.3, B4.7–B4.11, B7.4–B7.6, C1.1–C1.7, C1.9 and C2.1(ii)–C5.4.

N4.3 Subject to PD 61 § 3.7, C1.8 of the Guide also applies to claims in rem.

N4.4 After an acknowledgement of service has been filed a claim in rem follows the procedure applicable to a claim proceeding in the Commercial Court, save that the Claimant is allowed 75 days in which to serve particulars of claim: PD 61 § 3.10.

N4.5 PD 6.2 provides that the Admiralty Registrar will issue a direction allocating a claim form to the Admiralty Judge or to the Admiralty Registrar or to another Court. She or he is required to take into account, among other things, the sums in dispute. At present claims in excess of about £1 million are allocated to the Judge. Personal injury claims which involve no Admiralty expertise are transferred to the Claimant's County Court or, if appropriate, to the Queen's Bench Division.

N.5 The early stages of a Collision Claim

N5.0 Any party, or potential party, to a collision claim, who has in its control any electronic track data (as defined in rule 61.1(2)(m)) recording the tracks of the vessels involved leading up to the collision, should have regard to Appendix 13 ('Electronic Track Data in Collision Claims'), which contains provisions relating to (i) the preservation, pre-action disclosure and inspection, and early disclosure and

Section N   Admiralty

inspection, of electronic track data, and (ii) the case management of collision claims where electronic track data is available. (See also rule 61.4(4A) and PD 61 §4.7.)

N5.1 Where a collision claim is commenced in rem, the general procedure applicable to claims in rem applies subject to rule 61.4 and PD 61 §§ 4.1–4.7.

N5.2 Where a collision claim is not commenced in rem the general procedure applicable to claims proceeding in the Commercial Court applies subject to rule 61.4 and PD 61 §§ 4.1–4.7.

N5.3 Service of a claim form out of the jurisdiction in a collision claim (other than a claim in rem) is permitted in the circumstances identified in rule 61.4(7) only and the procedure set out in Appendix 9 of the Guide should be adapted accordingly.

N5.4 One particular feature of a collision action is that the parties must prepare and file a Collision Statement of Case. Prior to the coming into force of CPR Part 61, a Collision Statement of Case was known as a Preliminary Act and the law relating to Preliminary Acts continues to apply to Collision Statements of Case: PD 61 § 4.5.

N5.5 The provisions at C1.1 apply to part 2 of a Collision Statement of Case (but not to part 1).

N5.6 Every party is required, so far as it is able, to provide full and complete answers to the questions contained in part 1 of the Collision Statement of Case. The answers should descend to a reasonable level of particularity.

N5.7 The answers to the questions contained in part 1, formerly known as the preliminary act, are treated as admissions made by the party answering the questions. Leave to amend such answers can be sought but such leave will not lightly be granted and any such application will be subjected to close scrutiny; see The Topaz [2003] 2 Lloyd's Rep. 19. Amendments which would undermine the principles underpinning the answers to the questions contained in part 1 are likely to be refused otherwise than under the most special or exceptional circumstances; see Nautical Challenge v Evergreen Marine [2016] EWHC 1093 (QB).

Section N Admiralty

N.6 The early stages of a Limitation Claim

N6.1 The procedure governing the early stages of a limitation claim differs significantly from the procedure relating to other claims and is contained in rule 61.11 and PD 61 § 10.1.

N6.2 Service of a limitation claim form out of the jurisdiction is permitted in the circumstances identified in rule 61.11 (5) only and the procedure set out in Appendix 9 of the Guide should be adapted accordingly.

N.7 E-filing

N7.1 The issue of an Admiralty claim form, the issue of a notice requiring a caution against release and the issue of any other document must, since 25 April 2017, be done electronically.

N7.2 The electronic filing of such documents takes effect from the time at which the document was filed.

N.8 Case Management

N8.1 The case management provisions of the Guide apply to Admiralty claims save that

(a) In Admiralty claims the case management provisions of the Guide are supplemented by PD 61 § § 2.1–2.3 which make provision for the early classification and streaming of cases;

(b) In a collision case the claimant should apply for a Case Management Conference within 7 days after the last Collision Statement of Case is filed: PD 61 § 4.6;

(c) In a limitation claim where the right to limit is not admitted and the claimant seeks a general limitation decree, the claimant must, within 7 days after the date of the filing of the defence of the defendant last served or the expiry of the time for doing so, apply to the Admiralty Registrar for a Case Management Conference: PD 61 § 10.7;

(d) In a collision claim (PD 61 § 4.6) or a limitation claim a mandatory Case Management Conference will normally take place on

Section N   Admiralty

the first available date 5 weeks after the date when the claimant is required to take steps to fix a date for the Case Management Conference;

(e) In a limitation claim, case management directions are initially given by the Registrar: PD 61 § 10.8;

(f) In the Admiralty Court, the case management information sheet should be in the form in Appendix 2 of this Guide but should also include the following questions

1. Do any of the issues contained in the List of Common Ground and Issues involve questions of navigation or other particular matters of an essentially Admiralty nature which require the trial to be before the Admiralty Judge?
2. Is the case suitable to be tried before a Deputy Judge nominated by the Admiralty Judge?
3. Do you consider that the Court should sit with nautical or other assessors? If you intend to ask that the Court sit with one or more assessors who is not a Trinity Master, please state the reasons for such an application.

(g) In a collision claim where electronic track data is available the Court will seek to adopt fast track procedures for the determination of issues of liability as part of its duty actively to manage cases in accordance with the overriding objective, which may include making one or more of the directions listed in PD 61 §4.7: see also section N5.0 and Appendix 13 ('Electronic Track Data in Collision Claims');

(h) In a collision claim, the case management information sheet should also include the following question:
Do you or any other party have in their control electronic track data (as defined in rule 61.1(2)(m)) recording the tracks of the vessels involved leading up to the collision? If so, would it be appropriate for the Court to make one or more of the directions listed in PD 61 §4.7 (or other similar directions)? Please state reasons.

N.9   Evidence

N9.1 In collision claims, H1.6 and Appendix 4 are subject to the proviso that experience has shown that it is usually desirable for the main

Section N   Admiralty

elements of a witness' evidence in chief to be adduced orally. In collision claims where electronic track data is available it may be appropriate to (i) limit witnesses to those most closely involved with the collision, (ii) dispensing with oral evidence, and/or dispensing with an oral hearing: PD 61 §4.7(b), (e) and (g).

Authenticity

N9.2 **(a)** Where the authenticity of any document disclosed to a party is not admitted, that party must serve notice that the document must be proved at trial in accordance with rule 32.19. Such notice must be served by the latest date for serving witness statements or within 7 days of disclosure of the document, whichever is later.

(b) Where, apart from the authenticity of the document itself, the date upon which a document or an entry in it is stated to have been made or the person by whom the document states that it or any entry in it was made or any other feature of the document is to be challenged at the trial on grounds which may require a witness to be called at the trial to support the contents of the document, such challenge

   (i)   must be raised in good time in advance of the trial to enable such witness or witnesses to be called;
   (ii) the grounds of challenge must be explicitly identified in the skeleton argument or outline submissions in advance of the trial.

(c) Where, due to the late disclosure of a document it or its contents or character cannot practicably be challenged within the time limits prescribed in (a) or (b), the challenge may only be raised with the permission of the Court and having regard to the overriding objective (rule 1.1).

Skeleton arguments in Collision Claims

N9.3 In collision claims the skeleton argument of each party must be accompanied by a plot or plots of that party's case or alternative cases as to the navigation of vessels during and leading to the collision. All plots must contain a sufficient indication of the assumptions used in the preparation of the plot.

Section N   Admiralty

N.10   Split trials, accounts, enquiries and enforcement

N10.1 In collision claims it is usual for liability to be tried first and for the assessment of damages and interest to be referred to the Admiralty Registrar.

N10.2 Where the Admiralty Court refers an account, enquiry or enforcement, it will usually refer the matter to the Admiralty Registrar.

N.11   Release of vessels out of hours

N11.1 This section makes provision for release from arrest when the Registry is closed.

N11.2 An application for release under rule 61.8(4)(c) or (d) may, when the Registry is closed, be made in, and only in, the following manner:

    (a) The solicitor for the arrestor or the other party applying must telephone the security staff at the Royal Courts of Justice (020 7947 6260) and ask to be contacted by the Admiralty Marshal, who will then respond as soon as practically possible;

    (b) The solicitor for the arrestor or the other party applying must also file electronically his instructions for release and her or his undertaking to pay the fees and expenses of the Admiralty marshal as required in Form No.ADM12;

    (c) The solicitor must also file electronically written consent to the release from all persons who have entered cautions against release (and from the arrestor if the arrestor is not the party applying);

    (d) Upon being contacted by the Admiralty Marshal the solicitor must confirm that she or he has filed the documents in (b) and (c) above;

    (e) Upon the Admiralty Marshal being satisfied that no cautions against release are in force, or that all persons who have entered cautions against release, and if necessary the arrestor, have given their written consent to the release, the Admiralty Marshal shall effect the release as soon as is practicable.

N11.3 Practitioners should note that the Admiralty Marshal is not formally on call and therefore at times may not be available to assist. Similarly the practicalities of releasing a ship in some localities may

Section N   Admiralty

involve the services of others who may not be available outside Court hours.

N11.4 This service is offered to practitioners for use during reasonable hours and on the basis that if the Admiralty Marshal is available and can be contacted the Marshal will use her or his best endeavours to effect instructions to release but without guarantee as to their success.

N.12   Insurance of arrested property

N12.1 The Marshal will not insure any arrested property for the benefit of parties at any time during the period of arrest (whether before or after the filing of an application for sale, if any).

N12.2 The Marshal will use her or his best endeavours (but without any legal liability for failure to do so) to advise all parties known to the Marshal as being on the record in actions in rem against the arrested property, including those who have filed cautions against release of that property, before any such property moves or is moved beyond the area covered by the usual port risks policy.

N12.3 In these circumstances, practitioners' attention is drawn to the necessity of considering the questions of insuring against port risks for the amount of their clients' interest in any property arrested in an Admiralty action and the inclusion in any policy of a "Held Covered" clause in case the ship moves or is moved outside the area covered by the usual port risks policy. The usual port risks policy provides, among other things, for a ship to be moved or towed from one berth to another up to a distance of five miles within the port where she is lying.

N.13   Assessors

N13.1 In collision claims and other cases involving issues of navigation and seamanship, the Admiralty Court usually sits with assessors. The parties are not permitted to call expert evidence on such matters without the leave of the Court: rule 61.13. In collision claims where electronic track data is available it may be appropriate to limit the assistance to that of a single assessor, or to dispense with the assistance of assessors entirely: PD 61 § 4.7(f).

Section N Admiralty

N13.2 Parties are reminded of the practice with regard to the disclosure of any answers to the Court's questions and the opportunity for comment on them as set out in the Judgment of Gross J. in The Global Mariner [2005] 1 Lloyd's Rep 699 at p702.

N13.3 Provision is made in rule 35.15 for assessors' remuneration. Guidance as to assessors' remuneration in Admiralty cases is provided by Teare J in Practice Note dated 3 January 2017. The usual practice is for the Court to seek an undertaking from the claimant to pay the remuneration on demand after the case has concluded.

Section O
Arbitration

O.1 Arbitration claims

O1.1 (a) Applications to the Court under the Arbitration Acts 1950–1996 and other applications relating to arbitrations are known as "arbitration claims".

(b) The procedure applicable to arbitration claims is to be found in CPR Part 62 and its associated practice direction. Separate provision is made:

   (i) by Section I for claims relating to arbitrations to which the Arbitration Act 1996 applies;
   (ii) by Section II for claims relating to arbitrations to which the Arbitration Acts 1950–1979 ("the old law") apply; and
   (iii) by Section III for enforcement proceedings.

(c) For a full definition of the expression "arbitration claim" see rule 62.2(1) (claims under the 1996 Act) and rule 62.11(2) (claims under the old law).

(d) CPR Part 58 applies to arbitration claims in the Commercial Court insofar as no specific provision is made by CPR Part 62: rule 62.1(3).

Claims under the Arbitration Act 1996

O.2 Starting an arbitration claim

O2.1 Subject to O2.3 an arbitration claim must be started by the issue of an arbitration claim form in accordance with the CPR Part 8 procedure: rule 62.3(1).

O2.2 The claim form must be substantially in the form set out in Appendix A to practice direction 62: PD 62 § 2.2.

O2.3 An application to stay proceedings under section 9 of the Arbitration Act 1996 must be made by application notice in the proceedings: rule 62.3(2).

O2.4 Where a question arises as to whether an arbitration agreement is null and void, inoperative or incapable of being performed the Court may deal with it in the same way as provided by rule 62.8(3) which applies where a question arises as to whether an arbitration agreement has been concluded or the dispute which is the subject matter of the proceedings falls within the terms of such an agreement.

O.3 The arbitration claim form

O3.1 The arbitration claim form must contain, among other things, a concise statement of the remedy claimed and, if an award is challenged, the grounds for that challenge: rule 62.4(1).

O3.2 Reference in the arbitration claim form to a witness statement or affidavit filed in support of the claim is not sufficient to comply with the requirements of rule 62.4(1).

O.4 Service of the arbitration claim form

O4.1 An arbitration claim form issued in the Admiralty & Commercial Registry must be served by the claimant.

O4.2 (a) The rules governing service of the claim form are set out in CPR Part 6.
(b) Unless the Court orders otherwise an arbitration claim form must be served on the defendant within 1 month from the date of issue: rule 62.4(2). An application for an extension of this period will generally be considered without a hearing.

O4.3 (a) An arbitration claim form may be served out of the jurisdiction with the permission of the Court: rule 62.5(1).
(b) Rules 6.40–6.46 apply to the service of an arbitration claim form out of the jurisdiction: rule 62.5(3).

Section O   Arbitration

O4.4 The Court may exercise its power under rules 6.15 to permit service of an arbitration claim form on a party at the address of the solicitor or other representative acting for the party in the arbitration: PD 62 § 3.1. See also the Court's power under rule 6.37(5)(b).

O4.5 The claimant must file a certificate of service within 7 days of serving the arbitration claim form: PD 62 § 3.2.

O.5 Acknowledgment of service

O5.1 (a) A defendant must file an acknowledgment of service of the arbitration claim form in every case: rule 58.6(1).

(b) An adapted version of practice form **N210(CC)** (acknowledgment of service of a CPR Part 8 claim form) has been approved for use in the Commercial Court.

O5.2 The time for filing an acknowledgment of service is calculated from the service of the arbitration claim form.

O.6 Standard directions

O6.1 The directions set out in PD 62 § 6.2–6.7 apply unless the Court orders otherwise.

O6.2 An arbitration claim will be case managed, where necessary adapting the case management procedures provided throughout this Guide.

O6.3 The claimant should apply for a hearing date as soon as possible after issuing an arbitration claim form or (in the case of an appeal) obtaining permission to appeal.

O6.4 A defendant who wishes to rely on evidence in opposition to the claim must file and serve its evidence within 21 days after the date by which it was required to acknowledge service: PD 62 § 6.2.

O6.5 A claimant who wishes to rely on evidence in response to evidence served by the defendant must file and serve its evidence within 7 days after the service of the defendant's evidence: PD 62 § 6.3.

O6.6 An application for directions in a pending arbitration claim should be made by application notice under CPR Part 23. The timetable

Section O Arbitration

requirements for evidence in relation to an application notice under CPR Part 23 are those provided in section F. Where an arbitration application involves recognition and/or enforcement of an agreement to arbitrate and that application is challenged on the grounds that the parties to the application were not bound by an agreement to arbitrate, it will usually be necessary for the Court to resolve that issue in order to determine the application. For this purpose it may be necessary for there to be disclosure of documents and/or factual and/or expert evidence. In that event, it is the responsibility of those advising the applicant to liaise with the other party and to arrange with the Listing Office for a Case Management Conference to be listed as early as possible to enable the Court to give directions as to the steps to be taken before the hearing of the application.

O6.7 PD 62 § 6.6 and 6.7 provide for the Claimant's skeleton argument to be served not later than 2 days before the hearing date and the Respondent's skeleton argument to be served not later than the day before the hearing date. However:

(a) In relation to hearings of appeals in which permission to appeal has been granted, see O8.2 and in relation to applications under section 68 see O8.5;

(b) Where an application (other than one mentioned in (a) above) is likely to last more than half a day the Respondent's skeleton should be served one clear day before the hearing date, consistently with the Commercial Court practice for heavy applications. The parties should liaise to ensure this is possible.

O.7 Interim remedies

O7.1 An application for an interim remedy under section 44 of the Arbitration Act 1996 must be made in an arbitration claim form: PD 62 § 8.1.

O.8 Challenging the award

Challenge by way of appeal

O8.1 All applications for permission to appeal should comply with PD 62 § 12 which requires that:

Section O Arbitration

(a) Where a party seeks permission to appeal to the Court on a question of law arising out of an arbitration award, the arbitration claim form must, in addition to complying with rule 62.4(1)—

  (i) identify the question of law;
  (ii) state the grounds (but not the argument) on which the party challenges the award and contends that permission should be given;
  (iii) be accompanied by a skeleton argument in support of the application in accordance with paragraph 12.2; and
  (iv) append the award.

(b) Subject to paragraph (c), the skeleton argument—

  (i) must be printed in minimum 12 point font, with 1.5 line spacing,
  (ii) should not exceed 15 pages in length and
  (iii) must contain an estimate of how long the Court is likely to need to deal with the application on the documents.

(c) If the skeleton argument exceeds 15 pages in length the author must write to the Court explaining why that is necessary, and what increased length is required.

(d) Written evidence may be filed in support of the application only if it is necessary to show (insofar as that is not apparent from the award itself):

  (i) that the determination of the question raised by the appeal will substantially affect the rights of one or more of the parties;
  (ii) that the question is one which the tribunal was asked to determine;
  (iii) that the question is one of general public importance;
  (iv) that it is just and proper in all the circumstances for the Court to determine the question raised by the appeal.

Any such evidence must be filed and served with the arbitration claim form.

(e) Unless there is a dispute whether the question raised by the appeal is one which the tribunal was asked to determine, no arbitration documents may be put before the Court other than:

Section O   Arbitration

(i) the award; and
(ii) any document (such as the contract or the relevant parts thereof) which is referred to in the award and which the Court needs to read to determine a question of law arising out of the award.

("arbitration documents" means documents adduced in or produced for the purposes of the arbitration.)

(f) A respondent who wishes to oppose an application for permission to appeal must file a respondent's notice which:

(i) sets out the grounds (but not the argument) on which the respondent opposes the application; and
(ii) states whether the respondent wishes to contend that the award should be up held for reasons not expressed (or not fully expressed) in the award and, if so, states those reasons (but not the argument).

(g) The respondent's notice must be filed and served within 21 days after the date on which the respondent was required to acknowledge service and must be ac companied by a skeleton argument in support which complies with paragraph (b) above.

(h) Written evidence in opposition to the application should be filed only if it complies with the requirements of paragraph (d) above. Any such evidence must be filed and served with the respondent's notice.

(i) The applicant may file and serve evidence or argument in reply only if it is necessary to do so. Any such evidence or argument must be as brief as possible and must be filed and served within 7 days after service of the respondent's notice.

(j) If either party wishes to invite the Court to consider arbitration documents other than those specified in paragraph (e) above the counsel or solicitor responsible for settling the application documents must write to the Court explaining why that is necessary.

(k) If a party or its representative fails to comply with the requirements of paragraphs (a) to (i) the Court may penalise that party or representative in costs.

(l) The Court will normally determine applications for permission to appeal without an oral hearing but may direct otherwise, particularly with a view to saving time (including Court time) or costs.

Section O   Arbitration

- **(m)** Where the Court considers that an oral hearing is required, it may give such further directions as are necessary.
- **(n)** Where the Court refuses an application for permission to appeal without an oral hearing, it will provide brief reasons.
- **(o)** The bundle for the hearing of any appeal should contain only the claim form, the respondent's notice, the arbitration documents referred to in paragraph (e), the order granting permission to appeal and the skeleton arguments.

O8.2 If permission to appeal is granted, skeleton arguments should be served in accordance with the timetable for applications in section F.

Challenging an award for serious irregularity

O8.3   **(a)** An arbitration claim challenging an award on the ground of serious irregularity under section 68 of the 1996 Act is appropriate only in cases where there are grounds for thinking:

- (i) that an irregularity has occurred which
- (ii) has caused or will cause substantial injustice to the party making the challenge.

(b) An application challenging an award on the ground of serious irregularity should therefore not be regarded as an alternative to, or a means of supporting, an application for permission to appeal, or as a means by which to secure that an application for permission to appeal is dealt with at an oral hearing rather than on the documents.

O8.4 The challenge to the award must be supported by evidence of the circumstances on which the claimant relies as giving rise to the irregularity complained of and the nature of the injustice which has been or will be caused to the claimant.

O8.5 If the nature of the challenge itself or the evidence filed in support of it leads the Court to consider that the claim has no real prospect of success, the Court may exercise its powers under rule 3.3(4) and/or rule 23.8(c) to dismiss the application without a hearing. If a respondent considers that the case is one in which the Court could appropriately deal with the application without a hearing it should within 21 days file a respondent's notice to that effect together with a skeleton argument (not exceeding 15 pages) and any evidence relied upon. The applicant may file a skeleton/evidence in reply within 7 days of service of the respondent's notice and skeleton argument. Where the Court makes an order dismissing the application without a hearing the applicant will have the right to apply to the Court to set aside the order and to seek directions for the hearing of the application. If such application is made and dismissed after a hearing the Court may consider whether it is appropriate to award costs on an indemnity basis.

Skeleton arguments for the hearing of the challenge should be served in accordance with the timetable for applications in section F.

Multiple claims

O8.6 If the arbitration claim form includes both a challenge to an award by way of appeal and a challenge on the ground of serious irregularity, the applications should be set out in separate sections of the arbitration claim form and the grounds on which they are made separately identified.

O8.7 In such cases the documents will be placed before a Judge to consider how the applications may most appropriately be disposed of. It is usually more appropriate to dispose of the application to set aside or remit the award before considering the application for permission to appeal.

O.9 Time limits

O9.1 An application to challenge an award under sections 67 or 68 of the 1996 Act or to appeal under section 69 of the Act must be brought within 28 days of the date of the award: see section 70(3).

O9.2 The Court has power to vary the period of 28 days fixed by section 70(3) of the 1996 Act: rule 62.9(1). However, it is important that any challenge to an award be pursued without delay and the Court will require cogent reasons for extending time.

O9.3 An application to extend time made **before** the expiry of the period of 28 days must be made in a CPR Part 23 application notice, but the application notice need not be served on any other party: rule 62.9(2) and PD 62 § 11.1(1).

O9.4 An application to extend time made **after** the expiry of the period of 28 days must be made in the arbitration claim form in which the applicant is seeking substantive relief: rule 62.9(3)(a) and PD 62 § 11.1(2).

O9.5 An application to vary the period of 28 days will normally be determined without a hearing and prior to the consideration of the substantive application: PD 62 § 10.2.

Claims under the Arbitration Acts 1950–1979

O.10 Starting an arbitration claim

O10.1 Subject to O10.2 an arbitration claim must be started by the issue of an arbitration claim form in accordance with the CPR Part 8 procedure: rule 62.13(1).

O10.2 The claim form must be substantially in the form set out in Appendix A to PD 62 § 2.2.

O10.3 An application to stay proceedings on the grounds of an arbitration agreement must be made by application notice in the proceedings: rule 62.13(2).

O.11 The arbitration claim form

O11.1 An arbitration claim form must state the grounds of the claim or appeal: rule 62.15(5)(a).

O11.2 Reference in the arbitration claim form to the witness statement or affidavit filed in support of the claim is not sufficient to comply with the requirements of rule 62.15(5)(a).

O.12 Service of the arbitration claim form

O12.1 An arbitration claim form issued in the Admiralty & Commercial Registry must be served by the claimant.

O12.2 The rules governing service of the claim form are set out in CPR Part 6.

O12.3 **(a)** An arbitration claim form may be served out of the jurisdiction with the permission of the Court: rule 62.16(1).

(b) Rules 6.40–6.46 apply to the service of an arbitration claim form out of the jurisdiction: rule 62.16(4).

Section O   Arbitration

O12.4 Although not expressly covered by PD 62, the Court may in an appropriate case exercise its powers under rule 6.15 to permit service of an arbitration claim form on a party at the address of the solicitor or other representative acting for the party in the arbitration. See also rule 6.37(5).

O12.5 The claimant must file a certificate of service within 7 days of serving the claim form.

O.13 Acknowledgment of service

O13.1 (a) A defendant must file an acknowledgment of service in every case: rule 58.6(1).
(b) An adapted version of practice form **N210(CC)** (acknowledgment of service of a CPR Part 8 claim form) has been approved for use in the Commercial Court.

O13.2 The time for filing an acknowledgment of service is calculated from the service of the arbitration claim form.

O.14 Standard directions

O14.1 Where the claim or appeal is based on written evidence, a copy of that evidence must be served with the arbitration claim form: rule 62.15(5)(b).

O14.2 Where the claim or appeal is made with the consent of the arbitrator or umpire or other parties, a copy of every written consent must be served with the arbitration claim form: rule 62.15(5)(c).

O14.3 An application for directions in a pending arbitration claim should be made by application notice under CPR Part 23. The timetable requirements for evidence in relation to an application notice under CPR Part 23 are those provided in section F.

O.15 Interim remedies

O15.1 An application for an interim remedy under section 12(6) of the 1950 Act must be made in accordance with CPR Part 25.

Section O Arbitration

O15.2 The application must be made by arbitration claim form.

O15.3 A claim under section 12(4) of the 1950 Act for an order for the issue of a witness summons to compel the attendance of a witness before an arbitrator or umpire where the attendance of the witness is required within the district of a District Registry may be started in that Registry: rule 62.14.

O.16 Challenging the award

Challenge by way of appeal

O16.1 A party wishing to appeal against the award of an arbitrator or umpire must file and serve with the arbitration claim form a statement of the grounds for the appeal, specifying the relevant part(s) of the award and reasons: rule 62.15(6).

O16.2 A party seeking permission to appeal must also file and serve with the arbitration claim form any written evidence in support of the contention that the question of law concerns a term of the contract or an event which is not "one-off": rule 62.15(6).

O16.3 Any written evidence in reply must be filed and served not less than 2 days before the hearing of the application for permission to appeal: rule 62.15(7).

O16.4 A party who wishes to contend that the award should be upheld for reasons other than those set out in the award and reasons must file and serve on the claimant a notice specifying the grounds of its contention not less than 2 days before the hearing of the application for permission to appeal: rule 62.15(8).

O16.5 Applications for permission to appeal will be heard orally, but will not normally be listed for longer than half an hour. Skeleton arguments should be filed.

Claims to set aside or remit the award

O16.6 A claim to set aside or remit an award on the grounds of misconduct should not be regarded as an alternative to, or a means of supporting, an application for permission to appeal.

O16.7 The directions set out in PD 62 §§ 6.2–6.7 should be followed unless the Court orders otherwise.

Multiple claims

O16.8 If the arbitration claim form includes both an appeal and an application to set aside or remit the award, the applications should be set out in separate sections of the arbitration claim form and the grounds on which they are made separately identified.

O16.9 The Court may direct that one application be heard before the other or may direct that they be heard together, as may be appropriate. It is usually more appropriate to dispose of the application to set aside or remit the award before considering the application for permission to appeal.

O.17 Time limits

O17.1 (a) Time limits governing claims under the 1950 and 1979 Acts are set out in rule 62.15.
(b) Different time limits apply to different claims. It is important to consult rule 62.15 to ensure that applications are made within the time prescribed.
(c) The Court has power under rule 3.1(2) to vary the time limits prescribed by rule 62.15, but will require cogent reasons for doing so.

Provisions applicable to all arbitrations

O.18 Enforcement of awards

O18.1 All applications for permission to enforce awards are governed by Section III of CPR Part 62, rule 62.17.

O18.2 An application for permission to enforce an award in the same manner as a judgment may be made without notice, but the Court may direct that the arbitration claim form be served, in which case the application will continue as an arbitration claim in accordance with the procedure set out in Section I: rule 62.18(1) - (3).

O18.3 An application for permission to enforce an award in the same manner as a judgment must be supported by written evidence in accordance with rule 62.18(6).

Section O   Arbitration

O18.4 **(a)** Two copies of the draft order must accompany the application; one in Word format.
(b) If the claimant wishes to enter judgment, the form of the judgment must correspond to the terms of the award.
(c) The defendant has the right to apply to the Court to set aside an order made without notice giving permission to enforce the award and the order itself must state in terms:
  (i) that the defendant may apply to set it aside within 14 days after service of the order or, if the order is to be served out of the jurisdiction, within such other period as the Court may set; and
  (ii) that it may not be enforced until after the end of that period or any application by the defendant to set it aside has been finally disposed of: rule 62.18(9) and (10).

O.19   Transfer of arbitration claims

O19.1 An arbitration claim which raises no significant point of arbitration law or practice will normally be transferred:
(a) if a rent-review arbitration, to the Chancery Division;
(b) if a construction or engineering arbitration, to the Technology and Construction Court.

O19.2 Salvage arbitrations will normally be transferred to the Admiralty Court.

O.20   Appointment of a Commercial Judge as sole arbitrator or umpire

O20.1 Section 93 of the Arbitration Act 1996 provides for the appointment of a Commercial Judge as sole arbitrator or umpire. The Act limits the circumstances in which a Judge may accept such an appointment.

O20.2 Enquiries should be directed to the Judge in Charge of the Commercial Court or the Commercial Court Listing Office.

Section P
Miscellaneous

P.1   Out of hours emergency arrangements

P1.1   **(a)**   When the Listing Office is closed, solicitors or counsel's clerks should in an emergency contact the Clerk to the Queen's Bench Judge in Chambers by telephone through the security desk at the Royal Courts of Justice: PD 58 § 2.2.

(b)   The telephone number of the security desk is included in the list of addresses and contact details at the end of the Guide.

P1.2   When the Listing Office is closed an urgent hearing will initially be dealt with by the Queen's Bench Judge in Chambers who may dispose of the application or make orders allowing the matter to come before a Commercial Judge at the first available opportunity.

Appendix 1

Overriding Objective and Dedicated CPR Parts and Practice Directions

CPR 1.1 and 1.3

"1.1 (1) These Rules are a new procedural code with the overriding objective of enabling the court to deal with cases justly and at proportionate cost.
 (2) Dealing with a case justly and at proportionate cost includes, so far as is practicable –

   (a) ensuring that the parties are on an equal footing;
   (b) saving expense;
   (c) dealing with the case in ways which are proportionate –

   (i) to the amount of money involved;
   (ii) to the importance of the case;
   (iii) to the complexity of the issues; and
   (iv) to the financial position of each party;

   (d) ensuring that it is dealt with expeditiously and fairly;
   (e) allotting to it an appropriate share of the court's resources, while taking into account the need to allot resources to other cases; and
   (f) enforcing compliance with rules, practice directions and orders.

   ...

1.3 The parties are required to help the court to further the overriding objective."

Appendix I   Overriding Objective and Dedicated CPR Parts and Practice Directions

Dedicated CPR Parts and Practice Directions

Commercial Court: CPR Part 58 and PD 58
Admiralty Court: CPR Part 61 and PD 61
Arbitration: CPR Part 62 and PD 62
Financial List: CPR Part 63A and PD 63A
Shorter Trials Scheme and Flexible Trials Scheme: PD 51N
Electronic Working: PD 51O
Video Conferencing Guidance: Annex 3 of PD 32

Appendix 2
Case Management Information Sheet, Progress Monitoring Information Sheet and Pre-Trial Checklist

Case Management Information Sheet

The information supplied should be printed in bold characters

Party filing information sheet:
Name of solicitors:
Name(s) of advocates for trial:
[Note: This Sheet should normally be completed with the involvement of the advocate(s) instructed for trial. If the claimant is a litigant in person this fact should be noted at the foot of the sheet and proposals made as to which party is to have responsibility for the preparation and upkeep of the case management bundle.]

Preliminary:

(1) Is the case suitable for the Shorter Trials Scheme or the Flexible Trials Scheme in the interest of reducing the length and cost of trial?

(2) Please state whether the Case Management Conference (CMC) requires a High Court Judge or whether it is suitable for hearing by a Deputy High Court Judge.

Appendix 2 Case Management Information Sheet, Progress...

(3) If costs budgeting and costs management is applicable, do you consider that this CMC is an appropriate time to deal with those questions? Is this agreed between the parties?

Issues:

(4) Are amendments to or is information about any statement of case required? If yes, please give brief details of what is required.

(5) Can you make any additional admissions? If yes, please give brief details of the additional admissions.

(6) Are any of the issues in the case suitable for trial as preliminary issues?

Disclosure:

(7) Have reports been produced on disclosure of documents? If not, is it considered that they are unnecessary or disproportionate? Is this agreed?

(8) What form of disclosure is appropriate, and for what issues? Is this agreed?

(9) By what date can you give this form of disclosure?

(10) If a form of disclosure requiring a search is sought or agreed, do you contend that the search should be limited and if so in what way and why? Is this agreed?

(11) What (if any) use of IT is proposed to assist with disclosure? Has this been discussed between the parties?

(12) What timing and method is appropriate for inspection of documents? Is this agreed?

Evidence:

(13) **(a)** On the evidence of how many witnesses of fact do you intend to rely at trial (subject to the directions of the Court)? Please give their names, or explain why this is not being done.
(b) By what date can you serve signed witness statements?

Appendix 2   Case Management Information Sheet, Progress...

- **(c)** How many of these witnesses of fact do you intend to call to give oral evidence at trial (subject to the directions of the Court)? Please give their names, or explain why this is not being done.
- **(d)** Will interpreters be required for any witness? What arrangements may be necessary for the translation of witness statements?
- **(e)** Do you wish any witness to give oral evidence by video link? Please give his or her name, or explain why this is not being done. Please state the country and city from which the witness will be asked to give evidence by video link.
- **(f)** Are directions to be sought for permission for any of the witness statements to be more than 30 pages in length? If so, this will need to be justified by letter or skeleton argument.

(14)
- **(a)** On what issues may expert evidence be required?
- **(b)** What is the estimated cost of the proposed expert evidence?
- **(c)** Is this a case in which the use of a single joint expert might be suitable (see rule 35.7)?
- **(d)** On the evidence of how many expert witnesses do you intend to rely at trial (subject to the directions of the Court)? Please give their names, or explain why this is not being done. Please identify each expert's field of expertise.
- **(e)** By what date can you serve signed expert reports? Is this a case for sequential exchange of expert reports?
- **(f)** When will the experts be available for a meeting or meetings of experts? Is this a case for the experts to meet before reports?
- **(g)** How many of these expert witnesses do you intend to call to give oral evidence at trial (subject to the directions of the Court)? Please give their names, or explain why this is not being done.
- **(h)** Will interpreters be required for any expert witness? What arrangements may be necessary for the translation of reports?
- **(i)** Do you wish any expert witness to give oral evidence by video link? Please give his or her name, or explain why this is not being done. Please state the country and city from which the witness will be asked to give evidence by video link.
- **(j)** Might this be a case for any expert evidence to be taken concurrently at trial?

Trial:

(15) What are the advocates' present provisional estimates of (i) the minimum and maximum lengths of the trial (ii) the pre-reading time likely to be required for the Judge?

(16) What is the earliest date by which you believe you can be ready for trial?

(17) Is this a case in which a pre-trial review is likely to be useful?

(18) What use of IT is proposed at trial? Has this been discussed between the parties?

Resolution without trial:

(19) Is there any way in which the Court can assist the parties to resolve their dispute or particular issues in it without the need for a trial or a full trial?

(20) **(a)** Might some form of Alternative Dispute Resolution procedure assist to resolve or narrow the dispute or particular issues in it?
(b) Has the question at (a) been considered between the client and legal representatives (including the advocate(s) retained)?
(c) Has the question at (a) been explored with the other parties in the case?
(d) Do you request that the case is adjourned while the parties try to settle the case by Alternative Dispute Resolution or other means?
(e) Would an ADR order in the form of Appendix 3 to the Commercial Court Guide be appropriate?
(f) Are any other special directions needed to allow for Alternative Dispute Resolution?

(21) Has Early Neutral Evaluation been considered?

Other matters:

(22) What other applications will you wish to make at the CMC?

(23) Does provision need to be made in the pre-trial timetable for any application or procedural step not otherwise dealt with above? If yes, please specify the application or procedural step.

Appendix 2 Case Management Information Sheet, Progress...

(24) Are there, or are there likely in due course to be, any related proceedings (e.g. a Part 20 claim)? Please give brief details.

(25) Please indicate whether it is considered that the case is unsuitable for trial by a Deputy High Court Judge rather than a High Court Judge. If the case is considered to be unsuitable for trial by a Deputy High Court Judge please give reasons for this view.

(26) Please indicate whether it is considered that the case should be allocated to a designated Judge. If so please give reasons for this view and write to the Judge in Charge of the Commercial Court in accordance with D4.2.

[Signature of solicitors]

Note: This information sheet must be filed with the Commercial Court Listing Office at least 7 days before the Case Management Conference (with a copy to all other parties): see D8.5 of the Commercial Court Guide.

Progress Monitoring Information Sheet

The information supplied should be printed in bold characters

[SHORT TITLE OF CASE and FOLIO NUMBER]
Fixed trial date/provisional range of dates for trial specified in the pre-trial timetable:
Party filing information sheet:
Name of solicitors:
Name(s) of advocates for trial:
[Note: this information sheet should normally be completed with the involvement of the advocate(s) instructed for trial]

(1) Have you complied with the pre-trial timetable in all respects?

(2) If you have not complied, in what respects have you not complied?

(3) Will you be ready for a trial commencing on the fixed date (or, where applicable, within the provisional range of dates) specified in the pre-trial timetable?

(4) If you will not be ready, why will you not be ready?

[Signature of solicitors]

Note: This information sheet must be filed with the Listing Office at least 3 days before the progress monitoring date (with a copy to all other parties): see D12.2 of the Commercial Court Guide.

Pre-Trial Checklist

The information supplied should be printed in bold characters

[SHORT TITLE OF CASE and FOLIO NUMBER]

a. Trial date:

b. Party filing checklist:

c. Name of solicitors:

d. Name(s) of advocates for trial:

[**Note**: this checklist should normally be completed with the involvement of the advocate(s) instructed for trial.]

1. Have you completed preparation of trial bundles in accordance with Appendix 7 to the Commercial Court Guide?

2. If not, when will the preparation of the trial bundles be completed?

3. Which witnesses of fact do you intend to call?

4. **(a)** Which expert witness(es) do you intend to call (if directions for expert evidence have been given)?
   (b) Have the experts narrowed the areas of disputed expert opinion as far as possible?
   (c) If directions for expert evidence to be taken concurrently have not been made, will they be sought from the Judge at trial?
   (d) If this is or may be a case for expert evidence to be taken concurrently has there been a discussion between advocates as to the most suitable procedure: see H2.34 in the Commercial Court Guide?

5. Will an interpreter be required for any witness and if so, have any necessary directions already been given?

Appendix 2 Case Management Information Sheet, Progress...

6. Have directions been given for any witness to give evidence by video link? If so, have all necessary arrangements been made?

7. What are the advocates' confirmed estimates of (i) the minimum and maximum lengths of the trial (ii) the pre-reading time likely to be required for the Judge? (A confirmed estimate of length signed by the advocates should be attached)?

8. What is your estimate of costs already incurred and to be incurred at trial?

[Signature of solicitors]

Appendix 3
Draft ADR Order

1. On or before [*] the parties shall exchange lists of 3 neutral individuals who are available to conduct ADR procedures in this case prior to [*]. Each party may [in addition] [in the alternative] provide a list identifying the constitution of one or more panels of neutral individuals who are available to conduct ADR procedures in this case prior to [*].

2. On or before [*] the parties shall in good faith endeavour to agree a neutral individual or panel from the lists so exchanged and provided.

3. Failing such agreement by [*] the Case Management Conference will be restored to enable the Court to facilitate agreement on a neutral individual or panel.

4. The parties shall take such serious steps as they may be advised to resolve their disputes by ADR procedures before the neutral individual or panel so chosen by no later than [*].

5. If the case is not finally settled, the parties shall inform the Court by letter prior to [disclosure of documents/exchange of witness statements/exchange of experts' reports] what steps towards ADR have been taken and (without prejudice to matters of privilege) why such steps have failed. If the parties have failed to initiate ADR procedures the Case Management Conference is to be restored for further consideration of the case.

6. [Costs].

Note: The term "ADR procedures" is deliberately used in the draft ADR order. This is in order to emphasise that (save where otherwise provided) the parties are free to use the ADR procedure that they regard as most suitable, be it mediation, early neutral evaluation, non-binding arbitration etc.

Appendix 4
Standard Pre-Trial Timetable

1. [Form of disclosure, divided by issues] is to be made by [*], with inspection [*] days after notice. [Detail different forms of disclosure for different groups of issues where appropriate].

2. Signed statements of witnesses of fact, and hearsay notices where required by rule 33.2, are to be exchanged not later than [*].

3. Unless otherwise ordered, witness statements are to stand as the evidence in chief of the witness at trial.

4. Signed reports of experts
   (i) are to be confined to one expert for each party from each of the following fields of expertise: [*];
   (ii) are to be confined to the following issues: [*];
   (iii) are to be exchanged [sequentially/simultaneously];
   (iv) are to be exchanged not later than [date or dates for each report in each field of expertise].

5. Meeting of experts
   (i) The experts are to meet [before and] after reports by [*] [and by *];
   (ii) The joint memorandum of the experts is to be completed by [*];
   (iii) Any short supplemental expert reports are to be exchanged [sequentially/simultaneously] by not later than [date or dates for each supplemental report].

6. [If the experts' reports cannot be agreed, the parties are to be at liberty to call expert witnesses at the trial, limited to those experts whose reports have been exchanged pursuant to 4. above.]

Appendix 4 Standard Pre-Trial Timetable

[Or: The parties are to be at liberty to apply to call as expert witnesses at the trial those experts whose reports they have exchanged pursuant to 4. above, such application to be made not earlier than [*] and not later than [*].]

7 [The trial reading list for the Judge is to:

   (a) identify the issues that the Court will be asked to decide with the assistance of expert evidence;
   (b) in respect of each such issue, briefly state each party's case;
   (c) in respect of each such issue, identify the pages of the expert evidence that need to be read.]

8. The proposed use of IT at trial is as follows: []

9. Preparation of trial bundles in electronic or hard copy form (or part electronic, part hard copy) to be completed in accordance with Appendix 7 to the Commercial Court Guide by not later than [*].

10. The estimated length of the trial is [*]. This includes [*] pre-trial reading time.

11. Within [*] days the parties are to attend on the Commercial Court Listing Office to fix the date for trial which shall be not before [*].

12. The progress monitoring date is [*]. Each party is to provide a completed progress monitoring information sheet to the Commercial Court Listing Office at least 3 days before the progress monitoring date (with a copy to all other parties).

13. Each party is to provide a completed pre-trial checklist not later than 3 weeks before the date fixed for trial.

14. [There is to be a pre-trial review not earlier than [*] and not later than [*]].

15. Save as varied by this order or further order, the practice and procedures set out in the Admiralty & Commercial Courts Guide are to be followed.

16. Costs in the case.

17. Liberty to restore the Case Management Conference.

Appendix 5
Preparation of Skeleton Arguments

1. A skeleton argument is intended to identify both for the parties and the Court those points which are, and are not, in issue and the nature of the argument in relation to those points that are in issue. It is not a substitute for oral argument.

2. Skeleton arguments must therefore

    (a) make clear what is sought;
    (b) have regard to the List of Common Ground and Issues;
    (c) identify concisely:

    - (i) the nature of the case generally and the background facts insofar as they are relevant to the matter before the Court;
    - (ii) the propositions of law relied on with references to the relevant authorities;
    - (iii) the submissions of fact to be made with references to the evidence;

    (d) be in numbered paragraphs and state the name of the advocate(s) who prepared them;
    (e) avoid arguing the case at length;
    (f) be prepared in a format which is easily legible - no skeleton should be served in a font smaller than 12 point and with line spacing of less than 1.5;
    (g) comply with the limits on length to be found in this Guide or as ordered.

Appendix 6
Preparation of chronologies and indices

1. As far as possible chronologies and indices should not be prepared in a tendentious form and should be agreed.

2. The ideal is that the Court and the parties should have a single point of reference that all find useful and are happy to work with.

3. Common ground from the List of Common Ground and Issues should be included as appropriate.

4. Where there is disagreement about a particular event or description, it is useful if that fact is indicated in neutral terms and the competing versions shortly stated.

5. Chronologies and indices once prepared can be easily updated and are of continuing usefulness throughout the life of the case.

6. Chronologies and indices should be no longer than is necessary and should be cross referenced to the bundles.

Appendix 7
Preparation of Bundles (electronic or paper)

1. The preparation of bundles requires a high level of co-operation between legal representatives for all parties. It is the duty of all legal representatives to co-operate to this high level.

2. For the trial a **core bundle** should be provided **containing the really important documents in the case**. The documents in this bundle should be paginated, but each page should also bear its bundle and page number reference in the main trial bundles. It is particularly important to allow sufficient room for later insertions (see paragraph 3(viii) below). The core bundle should be prepared and provided at the latest by the time of the provision of the first trial skeleton. In an appropriate case, where all other bundles are in electronic form it may be convenient for there to be a core bundle that is in both handy-sized hard copy form and electronic form.

3. All bundles should be prepared as follows:

    (i) No more than one copy of any one document should be included, unless there is good reason for doing otherwise;
    (ii) Contemporaneous documents, and correspondence, should be included in chronological order;
    (iii) Where a contract or similar document is central to the case it may be included in a separate place provided that a page is inserted in the chronological run of documents to indicate:

    (A) the place the contract or similar document would have appeared had it appeared chronologically; and
    (B) where it may be found instead;

Appendix 7   Preparation of Bundles (electronic or paper)

- (iv) Documents in manuscript, or not fully legible, should be transcribed; the transcription should be marked and placed adjacent to the document transcribed;
- (v) Documents in a foreign language should be translated; the translation should be marked and placed adjacent to the document transcribed; the translation should be agreed, or, if it cannot be agreed, each party's proposed translation should be included;
- (vi) If a document has to be read across rather than down the page, it should be so placed in the bundle as to ensure that the top of the text is nearest the spine or left hand edge of the screen;
- (vii) Bundles that are printed in hard copy should (save where there is good reason otherwise) be printed/copied single-sided. No bundle should contain more than 300 (single-sided) pages;
- (viii) Bundles should not be overfilled, and should allow sufficient room for later insertions. Subject to this, the size of file used should not be a size that is larger than necessary for the present and anticipated contents;
- (ix) Bundles should be paginated, in the bottom right hand corner and in a form that can clearly be distinguished from any existing pagination on the document; the pagination should begin afresh at the beginning of each bundle;
- (x) Bundles should be indexed, save that a chronological bundle of contemporaneous documents need not be indexed if an index is unlikely to be useful;
- (xi) Bundles should be numbered and (where in hard copy) named on the outside and on the inside front cover, the label to include the short title of the case, and a description of the bundle (including its number, where relevant);
- (xii) Dividers or tabs within bundles may assist in the organisation and use of a bundle, but they should not be overused (for example to divide each individual page or piece of correspondence).

4. Documents within bundles should be marked as follows:

- (i) When copy documents from exhibits have been included in the bundle(s), then unless clearly unnecessary, the copy of the affidavit or witness statement to which the documents were exhibited should be marked in a convenient way (for example in the right hand margin or as a footnote, and in manuscript if need be) to show where the document referred to may be found in the bundle(s).

Appendix 7   Preparation of Bundles (electronic or paper)

- (ii) Unless clearly unnecessary, where copy documents in a bundle are taken from the disclosure of more than one party the documents should be marked in a convenient way (for example in the top right hand corner or as a footnote, and in manuscript if need be) to show from which party's disclosure the copy document has been taken;
- (iii) Where there is a reference in a statement of case or witness statement to a document which is contained in the trial bundles a note should be made in a convenient way (for example in the margin or as a footnote, and if necessary in manuscript) identifying the place where that document is to be found. Unless otherwise agreed this is the responsibility of the party tendering the statement of case or witness statement.
- (iv) Where the method of cross referencing used in (i) or (iii) above involves using electronic copies of statements of case or witness statements and has the effect of altering the format or length of the same as compared to the signed originals to which a statement of truth was applied, then a solicitor responsible for the production of the bundles must sign a short statement to confirm that he/she has checked and is satisfied that the wording of the statements of case or witness statements in the form appearing in the bundles remains unaltered from the wording in the signed originals to which a statement of truth was applied.

5. Large documents, such as plans, should be placed in an easily accessible file.

6. Save for documents in respect of which there has been a timely notice to prove authenticity, all documents in the trial bundle will be admissible in evidence without more. However the fact that documents in the trial bundle are admissible in evidence does not mean that all such documents have been adduced in evidence so as to form part of the evidence in the trial: see J8.5–8.7.

Appendix 8
Expert Evidence—Requirements of General Application

1. It is the duty of an expert to help the Court on the matters within the expert's expertise: rule 35.3(1). This duty is paramount and overrides any obligation to the person from whom the expert has received instructions or by whom she or he is paid: rule 35.3(2).

2. Expert evidence presented to the Court should be, and should be seen to be, the independent product of the expert uninfluenced by the pressures of litigation.

3. An expert witness should provide independent assistance to the Court by way of objective unbiased opinion in relation to matters within her or his expertise. An expert witness should never assume the role of an advocate.

4. An expert witness should not omit to consider material facts which could detract from her or his concluded opinion.

5. An expert witness should make it clear when a particular question or issue falls outside her or his expertise.

6. If an expert's opinion is not properly researched because she or he considers that insufficient data is available, this must be stated in her or his report with an indication that the opinion is no more than a provisional one.

7. In a case where an expert witness who has prepared a report is unable to confirm that the report contains the truth, the whole truth and

Appendix 8   Expert Evidence—Requirements of General Application

nothing but the truth without some qualification, that qualification must be stated in the report.

8. If, after exchange of reports, an expert witness changes her or his view on a material matter having read another expert's report or for any other reason, such change of view should be communicated in writing (through the party's legal representatives) to the other side without delay, and when appropriate to the Court.

9. All expert evidence – written or oral – should be as concise as possible.

10. An expert witness should be ready to take initiative to narrow the areas of disputed expert opinion as far as possible, including by initiating further dialogue between experts.

Please see also section H of the Commercial Court Guide.

Appendix 9
Service Out of the Jurisdiction: Related Practice

Service out of the jurisdiction without permission

1. **(a)** Before issuing a claim form or seeking permission to serve out of the jurisdiction, it is necessary to consider whether the jurisdiction of the English Courts is affected by the Civil Jurisdiction and Judgments Act 1982. Where each claim in the claim form is a claim which the Court has by virtue of the Civil Jurisdiction and Judgments Act 1982 power to hear and determine, service of the claim form out of the jurisdiction may be effected without permission provided that, in the case of service in Scotland or Northern Ireland, the relevant requirements of rules 6.32 and 6.34 are satisfied; and, in the case of service out of the United Kingdom, the relevant requirements of rules 6.33 and 6.34 are satisfied.

    These requirements include the requirement to file with the claim form a notice containing a statement of the grounds on which the claimant is entitled to serve the claim form out of the jurisdiction and to serve a copy of that notice with the claim form. In the case of service out of the jurisdiction of the United Kingdom, PD 6B § 2.1 requires the notice to be in the form of practice form N510 in order to comply with rule 6.34. Rule 6.34(2) provides that, if the claimant fails to file such a notice, the consequence is that the claim form may only be served once the claimant has filed the requisite notice or if the Court gives permission.

Appendix 9 Service Out of the Jurisdiction: Related Practice

(b) It is very important that the statement as to the grounds upon which the claimant is entitled to serve the claim form out of the jurisdiction is accurate and made with care. If entitlement to serve out of the jurisdiction without leave is wrongly asserted, a claimant may be ordered to pay the costs of a defendant's application to strike out the claim or set aside serve of the claim form on an indemnity basis.

(c) Rule 6.35 sets out the time periods during which a defendant must respond to a claim form where permission was not required for service, depending on whether the defendant is:

    (i) in Scotland or Northern Ireland;
    (ii) in a Member State or a Convention Territory; or
    (iii) elsewhere.

PD 6B § 6 sets out the periods for responding in the case of defendants served elsewhere. These provisions are subject to the modifications set out in rule 58 in relation to Commercial Court cases, including, but not limited to (i) that a defendant must file an acknowledgement of service in every case; and (ii) that the time periods provided by rule 6.35 apply after service of the claim form.

Application for permission: statement in support

2. (a) The grounds upon which a claimant may apply for the Court's permission to serve a claim form out of the jurisdiction pursuant to rule 6.36 (in circumstances where neither rule 6.32 nor rule 6.33 applies) are set out in PD 6B § 3.1.

  (b) An application for permission under rule 6.36 must set out:

    (i) the ground in PD 6B relied on as giving the Court jurisdiction to order service out, together with a summary of the facts relied on as bringing the case within each such paragraph;
    (ii) where the application is made in respect of a claim referred to in paragraph 3.1(3) of PD 6B, the grounds on which the claimant believes that there is between the claimant and the defendant a real issue which it is reasonable for the Court to try;
    (iii) the belief of the claimant that the claim has a reasonable prospect of success; and

Appendix 9   Service Out of the Jurisdiction: Related Practice

　　　　(iv) the defendant's address or, if not known, in what place the defendant is or is likely to be found.

　(c) The claimant should also present evidence of the considerations relied upon as showing that the case is a proper one in which to subject a party outside the jurisdiction to proceedings within it (stating the grounds of belief and sources of information); exhibit copies of the documents referred to and any other significant documents; draw attention to any features which might reasonably be thought to weigh against the making of the order sought; and otherwise comply with the duty of full and frank disclosure to the Court. Where convenient the written evidence should be included in the form of application notice, rather than in a separate witness statement. The form of application notice may be extended for this purpose.

Application for permission: copies of draft order

3.　The application must be accompanied by a draft order in Word format, and that draft must:

　(a) specify the periods within which the defendant must:

　　(i) file an acknowledgement of service;
　　(ii) serve or file an admission;
　　(iii) file a defence; and

　(b) set out any other directions sought by the claimant as to:

　　(i) the method of service;
　　(ii) the terms of any order sought giving permission to serve other documents out of the jurisdiction;

The relevant periods referred to in sub-paragraphs (a)(i)–(iii) above are specified in PD 6B § 6.1–6.6, and in the Table at the end of that Practice Direction.

Application for permission: copy or draft of claim form

4.　A copy or draft of the claim form which the applicant intends to issue and serve must be provided to the Judge. The endorsement to the

Appendix 9 Service Out of the Jurisdiction: Related Practice

claim form must not include causes of action or claims not covered by the grounds on which permission to serve out of the jurisdiction can properly be granted. Where the application is for the issue of a concurrent claim form, the documents submitted must also include a copy of the original claim form.

Arbitration matters

5. Service out of the jurisdiction in arbitration matters is governed by CPR Part 62. Rule 62.5 (3) applies rules 6.40–6.46 to the service of an arbitration claim form out of the jurisdiction under rule 62.5(1). The Judgments Regulation (recast) does not apply to "arbitration" (see Article 1(2)(d)), but what proceedings fall within the category of arbitration and what do not, may be a difficult question.

Practice under rules 6.32 and 6.33

6.
   (a) Although a CPR Part 7 claim form may contain or be accompanied by particulars of claim, there is no need for it to do so and in many cases particulars of claim will be served after the claim form: rule 58.5.
   (b) A defendant should acknowledge service in every case: rule 58.6(1).
   (c) The period for filing an acknowledgment of service will be calculated from the service of the claim form, whether or not particulars of claim are to follow: rule 58.6.
   (d) The periods for filing an acknowledgement of service and a defence are set out respectively in rule 6.35(2) (in relation to claim forms served in Scotland and Northern Ireland); in rule 6.35(3) (in relation to claim forms served pursuant to rule 6.33 on a defendant in a Convention Territory within Europe or a Member State); in rule 6.35(4) (in relation to claim forms served pursuant to rule 6.33 on a defendant in a Convention Territory outside Europe); and in paragraphs 6.1, 6.3, 6.4 and the Table in PD 6B in relation to claim forms served pursuant to rule 6.33 on a defendant in a country elsewhere: rule 6.35(5). See also rule 58.10(2).

Appendix 9 Service Out of the Jurisdiction: Related Practice

Practice under rule 6.36

7.   **(a)** Although a CPR Part 7 claim form may contain or be accompanied by particulars of claim, there is no need for it to do so and in many cases particulars of claim will be served after the claim form: rule 58.5. If the claim form states that particulars of claim are to follow, there is no need to obtain further permission to serve out of the jurisdiction: rule 6.38(2). However, permission must be obtained to serve any other document out of the jurisdiction: rule 6.38(1); other than in cases where the defendant has given an address for service in Scotland and Northern Ireland: rule 6.38(3).

(b) A defendant should acknowledge service in every case: rule 58.6(1).

(c) The periods for filing an acknowledgment of service will be calculated from the service of the claim form, whether or not particulars of claim are to follow: rule 58.6.

(d) The period for serving, and filing, particulars of claim (where they were not contained in the claim form and did not accompany the claim form) will be calculated from acknowledgment of service: rule 58.5(1)(c).

(e) The period for serving and filing the defence will be calculated from service of the particulars of claim.

8.   Time for serving and filing a defence is calculated:

(a) where the Particulars of Claim are served with the claim form, to be calculated by reference to the number of days listed in the Table in PD 6B plus an additional 14 days: PD 6B § 6.4.

(b) where the Particulars of Claim are served after the acknowledgement of service, 28 days from the service of the Particulars of Claim.

Practice under rules 6.40 to 6.44

9.   Where rules 6.40 to 6.44 refer to the Senior Master

(a) if permission is required for service out of the jurisdiction this must be obtained first before documents are forwarded to the Senior Master;

Appendix 9   Service Out of the Jurisdiction: Related Practice

   (b)   it is for the party to forward the documents to the Senior Master; and
   (c)   once documents have been forwarded to the Senior Master any questions about the progress of service should be directed to the Senior Master.

Other

10.   Attention is also drawn to the use of rule 6.15 (service of the claim form by an alternative method or at an alternative place) in an appropriate case.

Appendix 10
Security for Costs: Related Practice

First applications

1. First applications for security for costs should not be made later than at the Case Management Conference and in any event any application should not be left until close to the trial date. Delay to the prejudice of the other party or the administration of justice might well cause the application to fail, as will any use of the application to harass the other party. Where it is intended to make an application for security at the Case Management Conference the procedure, and timetable for evidence, for an ordinary application must be followed (see section F5 of the Guide).

Successive applications

2. Successive applications for security can be granted where the circumstances warrant. If a claimant wishes to seek to preclude any further application it is incumbent on the claimant to make that clear.

Evidence

3. An affidavit or witness statement in support of an application for security for costs should deal not only with the residence of the claimant (or other respondent to the application) and the location of its assets but also with the practical difficulties (if any) of enforcing an order for costs against it.

Investigation of the merits of the case

4. Investigation of the merits of the case on an application for security is strongly discouraged. It is usually only in those cases where it can

be shown without detailed investigation of evidence or law that the claim is certain or almost certain to succeed or fail will the merits be taken into consideration.

Undertaking by the applicant

5. In appropriate cases an order for security for costs may only be made on terms that the applicant gives an undertaking to comply with any order that the Court may make if the Court later finds that the order for security for costs has caused loss to the claimant and that the claimant should be compensated for such loss. Such undertakings are intended to compensate claimants in cases where no order for costs is ultimately made in favour of the applicant.

Stay of proceedings

6. It is not usually convenient or appropriate to order an automatic stay of the proceedings pending the provision of the security. It leads to delay and may disrupt the preparation of the case for trial, or other hearing. Experience has shown that it is usually better to give the claimant (or other relevant party) a reasonable time within which to provide the security and the other party liberty to apply to the Court in the event of default. This enables the Court to put the claimant to its election and then, if appropriate, to dismiss the case.

Appendix 11
Form of Freezing Order

adapted for use in the Commercial Court

** FREEZING INJUNCTION **

IN THE HIGH COURT OF JUSTICE
QUEEN'S BENCH DIVISION
COMMERCIAL COURT

Before The Honourable Mr Justice [   ]

Claim No.

BETWEEN

Claimant(s)/Applicant(s)

– and –

Defendant(s)/Respondent(s)

Appendix 11   Form of Freezing Order

PENAL NOTICE

If you [   ][1] **disobey this order you may be held to be in contempt of court and may be imprisoned, fined or have your assets seized.**

Any other person who knows of this order and does anything which helps or permits the Respondent to breach the terms of this order may also be held to be in contempt of court and may be imprisoned, fined or have their assets seized.

THIS ORDER

1. This is a Freezing Injunction made against [   ] ("the Respondent") on [   ] by Mr Justice [   ] on the application of [   ] ("the Applicant").

2. This order was made at a hearing without notice to the Respondent. The Respondent has a right to apply to the court to vary or discharge the order – see paragraph 13 below.

3. There will be a further hearing in respect of this order on [   ] ("the return date"[2]).

[4. If there is more than one Respondent-

    (a) unless otherwise stated, references in this order to "the Respondent" mean both or all of them; and
    (b) this order is effective against any Respondent on whom it is served or who is given notice of it.]

FREEZING INJUNCTION

[For injunction limited to assets in England and Wales]

5. Until after the return date or further order of the Court, the Respondent must not remove from England and Wales or in any way dispose of,

---

1 Insert name of Respondent(s).
2 In the Commercial Court, usually 14 days after the injunction was granted, particularly where parties are outside the jurisdiction.

Appendix 11 Form of Freezing Order

deal with or diminish the value of any of its, her or his assets which are in England and Wales up to the value of £

[For worldwide injunction]

5. Until the return date or further order of the Court, the Respondent must not—

    (1) remove from England and Wales any of his assets which are in England and Wales up to the value of £   ; or
    (2) in any way dispose of, deal with or diminish the value of any of his assets whether they are in or outside England and Wales up to the same value.

[For either form of injunction]

6. Paragraph 5 applies to all the Respondent's assets whether or not they are in its, her or his own name, whether they are solely or jointly owned [and whether the Respondent is interested in them legally, beneficially or otherwise].[1] For the purpose of this order the Respondent's assets include any asset which it, she or he has the power, directly or indirectly, to dispose of or deal with as if it were its, her or his own. The Respondent is to be regarded as having such power if a third party holds or controls the asset in accordance with its, her or his direct or indirect instructions.

7. This prohibition includes the following assets in particular—

    (a) the property known as [title/address] or the net sale money after payment of any mortgages if it has been sold;
    (b) the property and assets of the Respondent's business[2] [known as [name]] [carried on at [address]]] or the sale money if any of them have been sold; and

---

1 In the Commercial Court, usually 14 days after the injunction was granted, particularly where parties are outside the jurisdiction, and a Friday in the first instance.
2 Whether this wider wording should be included in relation to the Order and/or the provision of information will be considered on a case by case basis.

Appendix 11 Form of Freezing Order

(c) any money in the account numbered [account number] at [title/address].
(d) any interest under any trust or similar entity including any interest which can arise by virtue of the exercise of any power of appointment, discretion or otherwise howsoever.

[For injunction limited to assets in England and Wales]

8. If the total value free of charges or other securities ("unencumbered value") of the Respondent's assets in England and Wales exceeds £, the Respondent may remove any of those assets from England and Wales or may dispose of or deal with them so long as the total unencumbered value of its, her or his assets still in England and Wales remains above £.

[For worldwide injunction]

8.

(1) If the total value free of charges or other securities ("unencumbered value") of the Respondent's assets in England and Wales exceeds £, the Respondent may remove any of those assets from England and Wales or may dispose of or deal with them so long as the total unencumbered value of the Respondent's assets still in England and Wales remains above £.

(2) If the total unencumbered value of the Respondent's assets in England and Wales does not exceed £, the Respondent must not remove any of those assets from England and Wales and must not dispose of or deal with any of them. If the Respondent has other assets outside England and Wales, she, he or it may dispose of or deal with those assets outside England and Wales so long as the total unencumbered value of all its, her or his assets whether in or outside England and Wales remains above £.

PROVISION OF INFORMATION

9.

(1) Unless paragraph (2) applies, the Respondent must [within [] hours/days] of service of this order] and to the best of his ability inform the Applicant's solicitors of all its, her or his assets [in

Appendix 11   Form of Freezing Order

England and Wales] [worldwide] [exceeding £ in value[1]] whether in its, her or his own name or not and whether solely or jointly owned, giving the value, location and details of all such assets.[2]

(2) If the provision of any of this information is likely to incriminate the Respondent, she or he may be entitled to refuse to provide it, but is recommended to take legal advice before refusing to provide the information. Wrongful refusal to provide the information is contempt of Court and may render the Respondent liable to be imprisoned, fined or have its, her or his assets seized.

10. Within [ ] working days after being served with this order, the Respondent must swear and serve on the Applicant's solicitors an affidavit setting out the above information.[3]

EXCEPTIONS TO THIS ORDER

11.

(1) This order does not prohibit the Respondent from spending £ a week towards its, her or his ordinary living expenses and also £ [or a reasonable sum] on legal advice and representation. [But before spending any money the Respondent must tell the Applicant's legal representatives where the money is to come from.[4]]

---

1   This sub paragraph is designed for the business that is the business of the Respondent itself/herself/himself but carried on under a trading or business name. It is not designed for the business of a company with separate legal personality that is owned by a Respondent, and where the Respondent's property and assets comprise its/her/his interest in the company rather than the property and assets of the company.
2   Careful consideration must be given to inserting a realistic lower limit below which value assets need not be disclosed.
3   Careful consideration should be given to ensuring that this period is realistic having regard to the nature and volume of information that may be involved. It is not acceptable to invite the Court to impose unrealistic time limits, and costs orders may be made where this results in the party subject to the order having to bring the matter back before a Judge.
4   Consideration should also be given to amalgamating paragraphs 9 and 10 of the draft Order, so as to require only one disclosure exercise, verified by Affidavit.

Appendix 11 Form of Freezing Order

[(2) This order does not prohibit the Respondent from dealing with or disposing of any of its, her or his assets in the ordinary and proper course of business, [but before doing so the Respondent must tell the Applicant's legal representatives[1]].]

(3) The Respondent may agree with the Applicant's legal representatives that the above spending limits should be increased or that this order should be varied in any other respect, but any agreement must be in writing.

(4) The order will cease to have effect if the Respondent—

   (a) provides security by paying the sum of £ into Court, to be held to the order of the Court; or

   (b) makes provision for security in that sum by another method agreed with the Applicant's legal representatives.

COSTS

12. The costs of this application are reserved to the Judge hearing the application on the return date.

VARIATION OR DISCHARGE OF THIS ORDER

13. Anyone served with or notified of this order may apply to the Court at any time to vary or discharge this order (or so much of it as affects that person), but they must first inform the Applicant's solicitors. If any evidence is to be relied upon in support of the application, the substance of it must be communicated in writing to the Applicant's solicitors in advance.

INTERPRETATION OF THIS ORDER

14. A Respondent who is an individual who is ordered not to do something must not do it herself or himself or in any other way. She or he must not do it through others acting on her or his behalf or on her or his instructions or with her or his encouragement.

---

1 The proviso requiring advance notice should only be included where really necessary. It is not to be included otherwise.

Appendix 11 Form of Freezing Order

15. A Respondent which is not an individual which is ordered not to do something must not do it itself or by its directors, officers, partners, employees or agents or in any other way.

PARTIES OTHER THAN THE APPLICANT AND RESPONDENT

16. **Effect of this order**

    It is a contempt of Court for any person notified of this order knowingly to assist in or permit a breach of this order. Any person doing so may be imprisoned, fined or have their assets seized.

17. **Set off by banks**

    This injunction does not prevent any bank from exercising any right of set of it may have in respect of any facility which it gave to the respondent before it was notified of this order.

18. **Withdrawals by the Respondent**

    No bank need enquire as to the application or proposed application of any money withdrawn by the Respondent if the withdrawal appears to be permitted by this order.

[For worldwide injunction]

19. Persons outside England and Wales

    (1) Except as provided in paragraph (2) below, the terms of this order do not affect or concern anyone outside the jurisdiction of this Court.
    (2) The terms of this order will affect the following persons in a country or state outside the jurisdiction of this Court—

    (a) the Respondent or its officer or its, her or his agent appointed by power of attorney;
    (b) any person who–

    (i) is subject to the jurisdiction of this Court;
    (ii) has been given written notice of this order at it, her or his residence or place of business within the jurisdiction of this Court; and

Appendix 11 Form of Freezing Order

(iii) is able to prevent acts or omissions outside the jurisdiction of this Court which constitute or assist in a breach of the terms of this order; and

(c) any other person, only to the extent that this order is declared enforceable by or is enforced by a Court in that country or state.

[For worldwide injunction]

20. **Assets located outside England and Wales**

    Nothing in this order shall, in respect of assets located outside England and Wales, prevent any third party from complying with—

    (1) what it reasonably believes to be its obligations, contractual or otherwise, under the laws and obligations of the country or state in which those assets are situated or under the proper law of any contract between itself and the Respondent; and
    (2) any orders of the Courts of that country or state, provided that reasonable notice of any application for such an order is given to the Applicant's solicitors.

COMMUNICATIONS WITH THE COURT

All communications to the Court about this order should be sent to the Admiralty and Commercial Court Listing Office, 7 Rolls Building, Fetter Lane, London, EC4A 1NL quoting the case number. The telephone number is 020 7947 6826.
The offices are open between 10 a.m. and 4.30 p.m. Monday to Friday.

SCHEDULE A—AFFIDAVITS

The Applicant relied on the following affidavits—

[name]   [number of affidavit]   [date sworn]   [filed on behalf of]

(1)

(2)

SCHEDULE B—UNDERTAKINGS GIVEN TO THE COURT BY THE APPLICANT

(1) If the Court later finds that this order has caused loss to the Respondent, and decides that the Respondent should be compensated for that loss, the Applicant will comply with any order the Court may make.

[(2) The Applicant will—

  (a) on or before [date] cause a written guarantee in a form satisfactory to the Court in the sum of £ to be issued from a bank with a place of business within England or Wales, in respect of any order the Court may make pursuant to paragraph (1) above [and (7) below]; and

  (b) immediately upon issue of the guarantee, cause a copy of it to be served on the Respondent.]

(3) As soon as practicable the Applicant will issue and serve a claim form [in the form of the draft produced to the Court] [claiming the appropriate relief].

(4) The Applicant will [swear and file an affidavit] [cause an affidavit to be sworn and filed] [substantially in the terms of the draft affidavit produced to the Court] [confirming the substance of what was said to the Court by the Applicant's advocate].

(5) The Applicant will serve upon the Respondent [together with this order] [as soon as practicable]—

  (i) copies of the affidavits and exhibits containing the evidence relied upon by the Applicant, and any other documents provided to the Court on the making of the application;
  (ii) the claim form; and
  (iii) an application notice for continuation of the order.

[(6) Anyone notified of this order will be given a copy of it by the Applicant's legal representatives.]

Appendix 11 Form of Freezing Order

(7) The Applicant will pay the reasonable costs of anyone other than the Respondent which have been incurred as a result of this order including the costs of finding out whether that person holds any of the Respondent's assets and if the Court later finds that this order has caused such person loss, and decides that such person should be compensated for that loss, the Applicant will comply with any order the Court may make.

(8) If this order ceases to have effect (for example, if the Respondent provides security or the Applicant does not provide a bank guarantee as provided for above) the Applicant will immediately take all reasonable steps to inform in writing anyone to whom he has given notice of this order, or who she, he or it has reasonable grounds for supposing may act upon this order, that it has ceased to have effect.

[9] The Applicant will not without the permission of the Court use any information obtained as a result of this order for the purpose of any civil or criminal proceedings, either in England and Wales or in any other jurisdiction, other than this claim.]

[(10) The Applicant will not without the permission of the Court seek to enforce this order in any country outside England and Wales [or seek an order of a similar nature including orders conferring a charge or other security against the Respondent or the Respondent's assets].][1]

NAME AND ADDRESS OF APPLICANT'S LEGAL REPRESENTATIVES

The Applicant's legal representatives are—
[Name, address, reference, and telephone numbers both in and out of office hours and e-mail]

---

1 The proviso requiring advance notice should only be included where really necessary. It is not to be included otherwise.

Appendix 12
Electronic Working

The Electronic Working Scheme (CE-File) is in operation in the Commercial Court and the Admiralty Court. The Scheme is set out in Practice Direction 510

Please go to: https://www.justice.gov.uk/Courts/procedure-rules/civil/rules/part51/practice-direction-510-the-electronic-working-pilot-scheme

See also Practice Note to PD 510 – Paragraph 3.4(2)

When filing electronically, the following categories should be used. This will particularly help the Court deal with applications on the documents:

- Application.
- Witness Statement.
- Exhibit to Witness Statement (separate for each exhibit).
- Signed Consent Order (PDF).
- Draft Consent Order (Word).
- Draft Order (if not by consent) (Word).
- Correspondence.
- Other (only to be used if none of the above).

Email communication with the Judge through her or his Clerk is permitted where used responsibly but any such communication must always be copied to the other parties, and also (unless clearly unnecessary) copied to the Listing Office.

Appendix 13
Electronic Track Data in Collision Claims

Introduction

1. In many collision cases, the tracks of the vessels involved leading up to the collision(s) are captured electronically or digitally by, for example, ship or shore-based AIS, ECDIS, or voyage data recorders (such track data, and any associated visual or audio recordings, being referred to herein as "Electronic Track Data"; see rule 61.1(2)(m)). The availability of such Electronic Track Data can greatly aid the quick and efficient disposal of disputes over liability for the collision.

2. Where such Electronic Track Data is available, it may therefore be possible, and desirable, to modify or dispense with various aspects of the normal procedure in a Collision Claim. (The normal procedure in a Collision Claim is set out in rule 61.4, PD 61 §§4.1–4.6, and sections N.5, N.8, N.9 and N.14 of the Guide.)

Preservation of Electronic Track Data

3. Electronic Track Data will almost certainly be of great importance in any Collision Claim in which liability might be in dispute. A party to an anticipated Collision Claim should therefore take all reasonable steps promptly to preserve and/or procure the original and/or copies of any Electronic Track Data in its control. (Rule 31.6(2) provides that a party has a document "in his control" if (a) the document is in its physical possession, (b) it has a right to possession of the document, or (c) it has a right to inspect or take copies of the document.)

Appendix 13   Electronic Track Data in Collision Claims

Pre-Action Disclosure & Inspection of Electronic Track Data

4. It is to be expected that the early disclosure, and provision or inspection, of Electronic Track Data will enable the rapid and cost-effective resolution of many disputes, or potential disputes, concerning liability for collisions without recourse to formal proceedings.

5. Therefore, each party to an anticipated Collision Claim will generally be expected to

    a. disclose to one another any Electronic Track Data, which is or has been in its control, and

    b. if each party has Electronic Track Data in its control, thereafter exchange copies of and/or permit reciprocal inspection of such Electronic Track Data,

    during the course of pre-action correspondence. A failure by one party so to disclose, exchange copies of, or permit reciprocal inspection of, Electronic Track Data at the request of another party to an anticipated Collision Claim prior to the commencement of proceedings without good reason is likely to attract a costs sanction from the Court.

6. Furthermore, an application under rule 31.16 by a person likely to be a party to a subsequent Collision Claim for mutual or reciprocal disclosure and/or inspection of Electronic Track Data by another person likely to be a party to that action before proceedings have started is likely to be considered favourably by the Court if each such person has Electronic Track Data in its control.

Early Disclosure & Inspection of Electronic Track Data

7. Rule 61.4(4A) requires every party in a collision claim to give early disclosure of any electronic track data, which is or has been in their control, within either (a) 21 days after the defendant files their acknowledgment of service, or (b) where the defendant makes an unsuccessful application under CPR Part 11, within 21 days after the defendant files their further acknowledgment of service. Where every party has electronic track data in its control, each party must provide copies, or permit inspection of, that electronic track data within 7 days of a request by another party to do so: rule 61.4(4A).

8. The parties should then file at Court completed Collision Statements of Case in the usual way in accordance with rule 61.4. The time limits set out in rule 61.4 should not normally require extension because of the provision of Electronic Track Data pursuant to the paragraph above. (Rule 61.4 requires the parties to file at Court completed Collision Statements of Case (a) within 2 months after the defendant files its acknowledgment of service, or (b) where the defendant unsuccessfully applies under CPR Part 11 to dispute the Court's jurisdiction, within 2 months after the defendant files its further acknowledgment of service.)

Case Management when Electronic Track Data is available

9. In accordance with PD 61 §4.6, and paragraphs N8.1(ii) and (iv) of the Guide, the claimant should apply for a mandatory Case Management Conference within 7 days after the last Collision Statement of Case is filed, which mandatory Case Management Conference will normally take place on the first available date 5 weeks thereafter.

10. The availability of Electronic Track Data is likely to enable the Court to adopt fast track procedures for the determination of issues of liability in a Collision Claim. The Court will seek to adopt such fast track procedures as part of its duty actively to manage cases in accordance with the overriding objective, and will give due consideration to making one or more of the directions listed in PD 61 §4.7. (See also paragraphs N8.1(vii), N9.1 and N14.1 of the Guide.)

11. The parties should give careful consideration to the possibility of adopting such (or other) fast track procedures when completing their case management information sheets prior to the Case Management Conference: see paragraph N8.1(viii). Parties are reminded of their obligation to help the Court to further the overriding objective. While the Court will always be astute to manage each particular Collision Claim to meet the demands of justice and the overriding objective, in making directions for the proper management of the case, the Court will give due consideration to any agreement made by the parties designed to dispose of the claim in a swift and cost-efficient manner. (For example, reference is made to the Fast Track Procedure form of agreement prepared by the Admiralty Solicitors Group for use in Collision Claims where Electronic Track Data is available.)

Appendix 14
Guidance on location of hearing, and on transferring cases to/from Circuit Commercial Courts

Any decision on where a particular hearing or trial should take place, and any decision on whether a case as a whole should be transferred is for the Court rather than the parties. Cases which have a close connection with a region of England or with Wales and which do not have a significant international element may be particularly suitable for hearing outside London. This topic may be explored at a first Case Management Conference. As appears below, a case can remain in the Commercial Court (but on the basis that a Commercial Judge - a High Court Judge of the Commercial Court - is made available to conduct a substantive hearing or trial outside London) or be transferred to a Circuit Commercial Court (where a substantive hearing or trial may still be conducted at the Circuit Commercial Court by a Commercial Judge if a Commercial Judge is needed).

If a case remains in the Commercial Court but a hearing is more suitably held outside London, the Commercial Court will aim to enable a Commercial Judge to conduct the hearing outside London.

Further if a hearing outside London (in any Court, including a Circuit Commercial Court) needs a Commercial Judge, the Commercial Court will aim to provide a Commercial Judge to conduct the hearing.

If appropriate in the particular case, the case itself can be transferred to the Commercial Court. Where appropriate this may be on the basis that the substantive hearing or trial should be conducted outside London.

Enquiries should be directed to the Senior Listing Officer at the Commercial Court Listing Office. Where appropriate the matter can be discussed between the Judge in Charge of the Commercial Court and the relevant Designated Civil Judge or Circuit Commercial Judge.

Permission to transfer any case from the Commercial Court to a Circuit Commercial Court or vice versa may be granted only by a Judge of the Commercial Court.

In the case of a proposed transfer from a Circuit Commercial Court to the Commercial Court the parties should first inform the relevant Circuit Commercial Judge who can express a view; and an application should then be made to the Judge in Charge of the Commercial Court.

As to transferring cases from the Commercial Court to a Circuit Commercial Court:

1. If a case is suitable for transfer to a Circuit Commercial Court, either party can apply to the Commercial Judge prior to the CMC for transfer.

2. If the case is one that is suitable for transfer and a decision is made to transfer prior to the CMC, the Commercial Judge will order that the case be transferred to a Circuit Commercial Court and the CMC will take place at the Circuit Commercial Court.

3. If the case is one that is suitable for transfer and a decision is made to transfer at the CMC, the Commercial Judge will, in order to save the costs of a further hearing in the Circuit Commercial Court, usually make all the directions with the appropriate timetable down to trial in the same way as if the case were to remain in the Commercial Court, including a direction to fix the trial date through the appropriate listing officer (see paragraph 9 below) within a specified period of time. If, as is usually the case, it is thought desirable to give the parties time to try and settle the case through direct negotiation or ADR, this will be built into the timetable.

4. The Commercial Judge will consider the time at which transfer is to take place and this must be specified in the Order. The Commercial Judge will decide whether she or he considers a PTR or further CMC appears necessary.

5. The Order must be drafted by the parties in the usual way and filed with the Commercial Registry.

Appendix 14 Guidance on location of hearing, and on transferring...

6. Once the Order is sealed, the transfer from the Commercial Court is during normal circumstances effected by the Registry within one week; the transfer is effected by the Registry sending the Order to the Circuit Commercial Court. The Registry will also inform all parties on record once the case has been transferred.

7. The Circuit Commercial Court will then receive all the documents which were on the Commercial Court file and they will give the case one of their own numbers and inform the parties.

8. The case will then continue in exactly the same way as if at the Commercial Court save that the hearing date must be fixed with the listing office at the Circuit Commercial Court within the time limit specified in the Order. The parties must contact the specialist listing officer at the Court to which the case has been transferred. The telephone numbers and email addresses of the listing officers for the specialist list are:

London:
Tel: 020 7947 6826
E-mail: comct.listing@hmcts.gsi.gov.uk

Birmingham:
Tel: 0121 681 3160
E-mail: BPC.Birmingham@hmcts.gsi.gov.uk

Bristol:
Tel: 0117 366 4866/4833
E-mail: bristolmercantilelisting@hmcts.gsi.gov.uk

Leeds:
Tel: 0113 306 2441
E-mail: hearings@leeds.countycourt.gsi.gov.uk

Liverpool:
Tel: 0151 296 2445
E-mail: elizabeth.taylor@hmcts.gsi.gov.uk

Manchester:
Tel: 0161 240 5305
E-mail: manchester.mercantile@hmcts.gsi.gov.uk

Appendix 14   Guidance on location of hearing, and on transferring...

Newcastle:
Tel: 0191 201 2061
E-mail: helen.tait@hmcts.gsi.gov.uk

Wales:
Cardiff
Tel: 029 2037 6412
E-mail: amanda.barrago@hmcts.gsi.gov.uk

Mold
Tel: 01978 317406
E-mail: northwalescivillisting@wrexham.countycourt.gsi.gov.uk

Parties are asked to speak to the specialist listing officers who will tell them of the facilities available at other Courts.

9. The Commercial Court monitors compliance with its Orders through progress monitoring information sheets which have to be provided by the Progress Monitoring Date specified in the Order. The standard directions for the Circuit Commercial Courts provide for a Progress Monitoring Date; such a date should therefore be provided for in any Order. The Circuit Commercial Courts monitor progress in accordance with paragraph 8 of PD 59. A Pre Trial Review (either in Court or by telephone conference) may be held in the Circuit Commercial Courts if the parties make a request or the Circuit Commercial Judge so directs.

10. The parties are expected to keep the listing officer of the Court to which the case is transferred apprised of any settlement of the case. Where the Commercial Judge has not made all the directions or the parties need to make an application either orally or in writing, then the appropriate directions will be considered and made by the Circuit Commercial Judge.

Addresses and Contact Details

The Admiralty and Commercial Registry and Listing Offices and the Admiralty Marshal are at the following address:

7 Rolls Building, Fetter Lane, London EC4A 1NL

E-mail: comct.listing@hmCourts-service.gsi.gov.uk

DX 160040 Strand 4

The individual telephone numbers are as follows:

The Admiralty Marshal:
Tel: +44 20 7 947 7111

The Admiralty & Commercial Registry:
Tel: +44 20 7 947 6112

The Admiralty & Commercial Court Listing Office:
Tel: +44 20 7 947 6826

The Secretary to the Commercial Court Committee:
Mr Joe Quinn
Tel: +44 20 7 947 6826

Out of hours emergency number: (Security Office at Royal Courts of Justice): +44 20 7 947 6260.

Part 2
The Financial List Guide

Section A

General

1. Introduction

1.1 This is the general guide to the Financial List. The Financial List is a specialist list set up to handle claims related to the financial markets. It is situated in the Rolls Building in London and operates as a joint initiative involving the Chancery Division and the Commercial Court.

1.2 The objective of the Financial List is to ensure that cases which would benefit from being heard by judges with particular expertise in the financial markets or which raise issues of general importance to the financial markets are dealt with by judges with suitable expertise and experience.

1.3 Cases in the Financial List will be managed and heard by specialist judges so as to provide fast, efficient and high quality dispute resolution of claims related to the financial markets.

2. Jurisdiction

2.1 Claims in the Financial List may be commenced in the Commercial Court or the Chancery Division but the Financial List itself operates as a single list. The Chancellor of the High Court and the judge in the charge of the Commercial Court have joint overall responsibility for the Financial List.

2.2 CPR Part 63A defines the kinds of claims which may be brought in the Financial List. The definition involves three related but independent criteria. The first criterion relates to the subject matter of the claim as set out in rule 63A.1(2)(a). The defined subject matter is widely drawn but is subject to a requirement that the claim be for more than £50 million or equivalent. Even where that requirement is met the Financial List is not suitable for straightforward claims which

Section A   General

require no financial market expertise and such claims may be transferred out of the Financial List under CPR Part 30. The second criterion as set out in rule 63A.1(2)(b) is that the case requires particular expertise in the financial markets (as defined). The third criterion as set out in rule 63A.1(2)(c) is that the case raises issues of general importance to the financial markets (as defined). An example of the application of the second or third criterion could be to a case which relates to the defined subject matter but has a value lower than £50 million. If that case requires financial market expertise or raises issues of general market importance, it will be suitable for the Financial List. The criteria do not override provisions in statute or in the CPR which stipulate that particular cases must be issued in a particular division of the High Court, for example paragraph 1 of Schedule 1 to the Senior Courts Act 1981 (sale etc. of land).

2.3   The court has the general power to transfer proceedings into the Financial List under CPR Part 30. This permits the court to order cases into the Financial List which fall within the spirit but not the letter of the three criteria. Cases which fall outside the subject matter definition and/or the financial markets definition may nevertheless require comparable expertise or may be of comparable general importance. Thus, a case concerning insurance, re-insurance or professional negligence, or a case falling within the normal specialist jurisdiction of the Companies Court (insolvencies, capital reductions, schemes of arrangement as well

as shareholder disputes like unfair prejudice petitions and equitable petitions) will not generally fall within the definition of Financial List Claims but if issues arising in such a case were to require financial market expertise or were issues of general market importance, then it may be appropriate to issue the claim in the Financial List or transfer such a case or part of it into the Financial List.

3.   Financial List judges

3.1   Cases in the Financial List will be dealt with by specialist Financial List judges. Financial List judges are judges of the Chancery Division and the Commercial Court who have been authorised as such to hear and determine claims in the Financial List.

Section A General

3.2   Case management in the Financial List will be carried out by judges. That applies to claims issued in the Chancery Division as well as the Commercial Court.

4. Users' Committee

4.1   The Financial List has a Users' Committee which provides a forum in which the court can listen and respond to matters raised by litigators and others concerned with the financial markets. Membership of the committee includes the Financial List judges, representatives of regulatory bodies, general counsel and senior-in house litigation counsel, accountancy firms, City bodies, Market Associations dealing with financial matters, solicitors firms, COMBAR and the Chancery Bar Association. Anyone having views concerning the improvement of financial markets litigation is invited to make his or her views known to the Committee, preferably through the relevant professional representative on the Committee or its secretary.

Section B
Procedure in the Financial List

5. CPR Part 63A and Practice Direction

5.1 Proceedings in the Financial List are governed by the Civil Procedure Rules. Part 63A relates to the Financial List and the applicable Practice Direction is PD 63AA.

6. Designated judges and allocation

6.1 Proceedings in the Financial List will have a designated judge assigned to them at the time of the first case management conference. The designated judge will normally deal with all subsequent pre-trial case management conferences and other

hearings. Normally, all applications in the case, other than applications for interim payment, will be determined by the designated judge and he or she will be the trial judge.

6.2 The assignment of designated judges will be the joint responsibility of the Chancellor and the Judge in Charge of the Commercial Court. If the Claimant wishes to draw to the attention of the Chancellor and the Judge in Charge of the Commercial Court any aspect of the case which should be taken into account in deciding which judge to allocate, the Claimant should write to them (copied to the other parties) four weeks prior to the date fixed for the first Case Management Conference, briefly identifying the key issues in the case and any matters considered relevant. Such issues must relate to general rather than individual judge allocation, including whether and, if so, why, it is a considered to be more appropriate for a Commercial Court or a Chancery Division Financial List judge, bearing in mind that the standard procedure will be identical for all cases in the

Financial List. If practicable, this should be a joint letter agreed to by all parties. If not, the other parties should write with their own comments, copied to the other parties, three weeks prior to the date for the first Case Management Conference.

7. Applicability of other procedural guides

7.1 The Financial List will adopt a unified procedure, irrespective of whether the case was issued in the Chancery Division or the Commercial Court. This guide is the primary source of guidance for proceedings in the Financial List. For matters not dealt with in this guide nor in CPR Part 63A or Practice Direction 63AA, the Admiralty and Commercial Court Guide (ACCG) will apply. For any other issues not dealt with in those sources, the Chancery Guide will apply.

7.2 References in the ACCG to the Commercial List or the Commercial Court shall be treated as referring to the Financial List for claims in the Financial List. References in the ACCG to Forms shall be treated as referring to the equivalent approved Financial List Forms. References in the ACCG to interlocutory hearings being on Fridays and to trial days not including Fridays apply only to claims in the Financial List proceeding in the Commercial Court. Sections D.4 and N and O of the ACCG shall not apply to claims in the Financial List.

8. Transfers

8.1 Cases may be transferred into and out of the Financial List, if appropriate, in accordance with CPR Part 30 and Practice Direction 63AA paragraphs 4.1 and following.

9. Market test cases

9.1 The Financial List will conduct a pilot Financial Markets Test Case Scheme, to facilitate the resolution of market issues in relation to which immediately relevant authoritative English law guidance is needed without the need for a present cause of action between the parties to the proceedings.

Section B　Procedure in the Financial List

9.2 The pilot provides a mechanism for the court to grant declaratory relief in a "friendly action" because it is in the public interest to do so in accordance with the guidance provided in *Rolls-Royce plc v Unite the Union* [2009] EWCA Civ 387. Such actions will require there to be a set of facts against which the decision is to be made, which should, if possible, be agreed. The court will also need to be satisfied that all sides of the argument will be fully and properly put.

9.3 The general rule will be that there shall be no order as to costs. If it is considered that a different order may be appropriate this should be raised at the first case management conference.

9.4 The pilot is governed by CPR Practice Direction 51M.

Section C
General Arrangements

10. Issuing proceedings in the Financial List

10.1 Proceedings in the Financial List will be issued in the Rolls Building. They may be issued in the Commercial Court or the Chancery Division.

10.2 Within seven days of issue or confirmation of a new case number the Claimant must complete a Claim Information Form providing information about the nature of the claim and of the parties. This will enable the court to gather statistics which will be valuable for the future development of the Financial List.

11. Arrangements for listing

11.1 Arrangements for listing of cases in the Financial List will be made by the relevant listing office. For cases issued in the Chancery Division that is the Chancery Listing

Office and for cases issued in the Commercial Court that is the Commercial Court Listing Office.

12. Contact

12.1 The Financial List is situated in the Rolls Building at 7 Rolls Building, Fetter Lane, London EC4A 1NL.

12.2 For issuing proceedings and listing, contact the appropriate office in the Rolls Building:

Section C   General Arrangements

	Chancery Division	**Commercial Court**
Email:		
Issue: Listing:	chancery.issue@hmcts.gsi.gov.uk rcjchancery.judgeslisting@hmcts.gsi.gov.uk	comct.issue@hmcts.gsi.gov.uk comct.listing@hmcts.gsi.gov.uk
Telephone		
	Issue: 020 7947 7783 Issue fax: 0870 761 7719 Listing: 020 7947 7717, 020 7947 6690 Listing fax: 0870 739 5869	Enquiries: 020 7947 6112 Listing: 020 7947 6826 Fax: 0870 761 7725

12.3   The secretary of the Financial List Users' Committee is Vannina Ettori, Legal Adviser to the Chancellor of the High Court. She may be contacted at vannina.ettori@judiciary.gsi.gov.uk.

Part 3
The Circuit Commercial (Mercantile) Court Guide

1. **Introduction**

1.1 The Circuit Commercial Courts (formerly the Mercantile Courts) operate in eight regional centres throughout England and Wales as part of the Queens Bench Division of the High Court. They decide business disputes of all kinds apart from those which, because of their size, value or complexity, will be dealt with by the Commercial Court. As well as large cases, the Circuit Commercial Courts decide smaller disputes and recognise the importance of these, particularly to small and medium sized businesses. They form part of the Business and Property Courts of England and Wales.

1.2 This Guide explains how to conduct business cases in the Circuit Commercial Courts and it therefore concentrates on the distinctive features of litigation in these Courts. It is not a summary of or a substitute for the Civil Procedure Rules (CPR) which govern all civil cases. Nor does it replace Part 59 of the CPR which deals specifically with Circuit Commercial Courts, or its Practice Direction ("PD59"). But it is a guide to the practice of these Courts and may be cited, as appropriate, in any Circuit Commercial case.

1.3 By Part 59.1(2) a Circuit Commercial claim is one which "relates to a commercial or business matter in a broad sense". This covers most business disputes including cases about:

   (a) business documents and contracts;
   (b) the export, import, carriage and sale of goods;
   (c) insurance and re-insurance;
   (c) banking and financial services; guarantees;
   (d) markets and exchanges; sale of commodities;
   (e) share sale agreements;

Part 3 · The Circuit Commercial (Mercantile) Court Guide

- **(f)** professional negligence in a commercial context (e.g. accountants, financial intermediaries and advisors and solicitors);
- **(g)** business agency and management agreements;
- **(h)** restraint of trade;
- **(i)** injunctions affecting commercial matters, including post-termination of employment restrictions;
- **(j)** confidential information;
- **(k)** freezing and search orders; and
- **(l)** arbitration claims, in particular appeals on points of law from, and challenges to, arbitration awards made under the Arbitration Act 1996 and the enforcement of such awards.

1.4   It follows that the range of cases heard in the Circuit Commercial Court is wide. Provided that a case involves a dispute of a genuinely business nature which is fit for the High Court, the Circuit Commercial Court will usually accommodate it. All Circuit Commercial judges are authorised to try civil High Court cases generally and will usually accept actions at the margins of the Circuit Commercial definition into their courts.

1.5   Generally, cases in the Circuit Commercial Courts are heard by designated Circuit Commercial judges. Other judges with business experience also sit in the Circuit Commercial Courts. Details of each court and each judge are set out in Appendix A. As these details change please check the online version of this Guide before relying on them.

1.6   Circuit Commercial judges manage Circuit Commercial cases and deal with all interlocutory (ie pre-trial) applications. These are not heard by Masters or District judges (PD59 para.1.3(1)). Wherever possible, the trial judge will have dealt with the case at some or all of its earlier stages. This provides continuity and consistency. Once a judgment is obtained, enforcement applications are heard by Masters or District judges (PD59 para.1.3)

1.7   The Judge in charge of the Commercial Court is also the Judge in charge of the Circuit Commercial Courts. The Commercial Courts Guide may often be of relevance to a claim in the Circuit Commercial Court and supplements it. If a point is not specifically covered in this Guide, reference should be made to the Commercial Court

Part 3 The Circuit Commercial (Mercantile) Court Guide

Guide. However, practitioners should bear in mind that some parts of the Commercial Court Guide are only appropriate for very large cases and there is a particular need to be proportionate in a Circuit Commercial case. Sometimes, the rules governing the two courts are different and these will be identified in this Guide.

1.8 A table of cross-references to relevant Rules, Practice Directions and the Commercial Court Guide is at Appendix E.

1.9 The Court's ability to meet the changing needs of the commercial community depends in part upon a steady flow of information and constructive suggestions between the Court, litigants and professional advisers. Each Circuit Commercial Court has a Users Committee. Users are encouraged to make the fullest use of this important channel of communication. Details of local users committees appear in Appendix A.

1.10 Although the Circuit Commercial Courts serve different regions in England and Wales, their

practices and approach are the same. There are some practical differences in their administration (for example listing) and these are explained in Appendix A.

1.11 The Circuit Commercial Courts seek to operate in a way which gives effect to the overriding objective of dealing with cases justly and at proportionate cost,, is streamlined, accessible to non-lawyers, promotes the early resolution of disputes wherever possible and actively manages through to trial those cases which do not settle.

1.12 It is incumbent upon the parties to help the Court to achieve the overriding objective. They should co-operate courteously to achieve resolution at the lowest feasible cost and in the shortest practicable time. They should put their cards on the table from the outset. The Court expects a high level of co-operation and realism from their legal representatives. It discourages over-lengthy or argumentative correspondence. Parties who fail to observe these and other requirements of the overriding objective can expect to be ordered to pay the unnecessary costs incurred. They must also respect and comply with the rules, practice directions and orders of the Court. They will face sanctions if they do not.

Part 3 The Circuit Commercial (Mercantile) Court Guide

2. Pre-Action Correspondence

2.1 The Practice Direction entitled "Pre-Action Conduct" (within White Book Vol.1 Section C "Pre-Action Conduct and Protocols) applies to actions in the Circuit Commercial Court. It should be observed, although it is sometimes necessary or appropriate to start proceedings without following the procedures set out there, for example, where there is urgency. There is no specific Pre-Action Protocol for the Circuit Commercial Court but some cases which may proceed in that court are covered by an approved protocol, such as the Professional Negligence Pre-Action Protocol. Subject to complying with the Practice Direction and any applicable protocol, the parties to proceedings in the Circuit Commercial Court are not required or expected, to engage in elaborate pre-action procedures, and restraint is encouraged.

2.2 Thus, the letter of claim should be concise and it is usually sufficient to explain the proposed claim and identify key dates and matters, so that the potential defendant can understand and investigate the allegations. Only essential documents need be supplied. A potential defendant should respond to a letter of claim concisely and again, only essential documents need be supplied.

3. Commencement and Transfer

Starting a case in the circuit commercial court

3.1 Except for arbitration applications which are governed by the provisions of Part 62, the case will be begun by a claim form under Part 7 or Part 8. All claim forms should be marked "CIRCUIT COMMERCIAL COURT" (outside London, and after the reference to the appropriate registry) or "LONDON CIRCUIT COMMERCIAL COURT". Failure to do this may result in non-allocation to that Court or delay in processing the claim. The claim form should be verified by a statement of truth.

3.2 Part8 Claims

These are appropriate only where there is no substantial dispute of fact, for example where the case turns on a pure point of law or the interpretation of a contract. All Part 8 Claims should be marked as such.

Part 3   The Circuit Commercial (Mercantile) Court Guide

3.3   Issue of Claim Forms

In every Court a party may request it to issue the Claim Form by attending in person or by post. In addition, in the London Circuit Commercial Court, a party may request it to issue the claim form electronically. This procedure, called CE-Filing, is accessed by going to the CE-Filing website at "http://www.ce-file.uk/; In order to use this system it is necessary to become a registered user first. Instructions for this and subsequent lodging of claim forms etc appear on the website. When issuing a claim form, please select the Business and Property Court dialog box first. Thereafter it will be possible to select the London Circuit Commercial Court option. Practitioners are encouraged to use this method of issue wherever possible. Further guidance is available in the User Guide accessible from the website along with PD51O also available on the website.

3.4   Particulars of claim and the claim form

Although particulars of claim may be served with the claim form, this is not a requirement in the Circuit Commercial Court. However, if they are not contained in or served with the claim form, (a) they must contain a statement that if an acknowledgment of service is filed indicating an intention to defend the claim, particulars of claim will follow and (b) the particulars of claim must be served within 28 days after the defendant has filed an acknowledgment of service indicating an intention to defend the claim: rule 59.4.

3.5   Service of the claim form

Claim forms issued in the Circuit Commercial Court are, as elsewhere in the High Court, served by the parties, not by the Court. Methods of service are set out in Part 6, which is supplemented by PD6A and 6B.

3.6   Applications for an extension of time in which to serve a claim form are governed by rule 7.6. The evidence required on such an application is set out in PD7A para.8.2. In an appropriate case it may be presented by an application notice verified by a statement of truth and without a separate witness statement: rule 32.6(2).

Part 3 The Circuit Commercial (Mercantile) Court Guide

3.7 When the claimant has served the claim form he must file a certificate of service: rule 6.17(2). This is required before a claimant can obtain judgment in default (see Part 12).

3.8 Acknowledgment of service

A defendant must file an acknowledgment of service in every case: rule 59.5. The period for filing an acknowledgment of service is calculated from the service of the claim form, whether or not particulars of claim are contained in or accompany the claim form or are to follow service of the claim form. Rule 9.1(2), which provides that in certain circumstances the defendant need not respond to the claim until particulars of claim have been served on him, does not apply: rule 59.5.

3.9 The period for filing an acknowledgment of service is 14 days after service of the claim form unless the claim form has been served abroad If it has been served out of the jurisdiction without the permission of the court under rules 6.32 and 33 the time for filing an acknowledgment of service is governed by rule 6.35. If the claim form has been served out of the jurisdiction with the permission of the court under rule 6.36 the time for filing an acknowledgment of service is governed by rule 6.37(5), See PD6B and the table to which it refers: rule 59.5 (3).

3.10 Service of the claim form out of the jurisdiction

Service of claim forms outside the jurisdiction without permission is governed by rules 6.32–6.35, and, where rule 6.35(5) applies, by PD6B. Applications for permission to serve a claim form out of the jurisdiction are governed by rules 6.36 and 6.37 and PD6B. A guide to the appropriate practice is set out in Appendix 9 of the Commercial Court Guide. Service of process in some foreign countries may take a long time to complete; it is therefore important that solicitors take prompt steps to effect service.

3.11 If the defendant intends to dispute the court's jurisdiction or to contend that the court should not exercise its jurisdiction he must file an acknowledgment of service (see rule 11(2) and issue an application notice. An application to dispute the court's jurisdiction must be made within 28 days after filing an acknowledgment of service: rule

59.6. If the defendant wishes to rely on written evidence in support of that application, he must file and serve that evidence when he issues the application. In an appropriate case it may be presented by an application notice verified by a statement of truth and without a separate witness statement: rule 32.6(2).

3.12 If the defendant makes an application under rule 11(1), the claimant is not bound to serve particulars of claim until that application has been disposed of: rule 59.6(3).

3.13 Effect of an application challenging the jurisdiction

An acknowledgment of service of a Part 7 or Part 8 claim form which is followed by an application challenging the jurisdiction under Part 11 does not constitute a submission by the defendant to the jurisdiction: rules 11(3) and 11(7).

3.14 Default judgment

Default judgment is governed by Part 12 and PD12. However, because in the Circuit Commercial Court the period for filing the acknowledgment of service is calculated from service of the claim form (PD59 para.5(2)), the reference to "particulars of claim" in PD12 para.4.1(l) should be read as referring to the claim form. In addition, if particulars of claim were not served with the claim form and the defendant then fails to acknowledge service, default judgment must be the subject of an application, not a request. It can be made without notice but the Court may direct its service on the defendant: rule 59.7.

Transfer of cases to and from a circuit commercial court

3.15 The procedure for transfer into the Circuit Commercial Court is set out in rule 59.3 and PD59 para.4. In respect of applications to transfer other than from the Commercial Court, these can be dealt with only by Circuit Commercial judges. A Circuit Commercial judge also has the power to transfer such a case into the Circuit Commercial Court of his own motion. If both parties consent to a such transfer into the Circuit Commercial Court, the application may be made by letter. Such applications should be made early in the proceedings.

3.16 If a party wishes to transfer the case from a Circuit Commercial Court to different specialist list other than the Commercial Court, only a judge of that specialist list may grant such transfer. The party seeking transfer should refer the matter first to the Circuit Commercial judge because if he considers that transfer is appropriate the judge of the relevant specialist list to which transfer is sought can be informed. In some cases (for example transfer to the TCC) the Circuit Commercial judge may also sit as a TCC judge and can permit the transfer directly.

3.17 Permission to transfer any case from the Commercial Court to the Circuit Commercial Court, or vice versa, may be granted only by a judge of the Commercial Court. Guidance about such transfers is contained in Guidance at Appendix 14 to the Commercial Court Guide.

3.18 In an appropriate case, it may be possible for a case commenced in a particular Circuit Commercial Court to be tried locally by a judge of the Commercial Court. If any party wishes the case to be so tried they should mention the matter to the Circuit Commercial judge at the earliest opportunity. The papers will thereafter be referred to the judge in charge of the Commercial Court together with any comments of the Circuit Commercial judge as to the appropriateness of trial before a Commercial Court judge. If the judge in charge agrees, the necessary arrangements will be made. In most cases, formal transfer into the Commercial Court (albeit with case management and trial locally) will not be required.

Shorter and flexible trials scheme

3.19 PD51N provides a procedure for shorter trials of no more than 4 days, with set, truncated directions and early hearing dates and for flexible trials with truncated directions agreed by the parties. Such directions include limited disclosure, witness statements which may be confined to particular matters and which in any event do not excess 25 pages without good reason, strictly controlled cross-examination at trial and judgment normally within 6 weeks. The purpose of both is to enable such disputes to be decided speedily and at lower cost. Such procedures are available in the London Circuit Commercial Court and may be particularly aposite for many claims

Part 3   The Circuit Commercial (Mercantile) Court Guide

in that court. A claimant wishing to start a claim within the Shorter Trials Scheme must mark the claim form "Queens Bench Division, London Circuit Commercial Court, Shorter Trials Scheme". If the defendant objects, this will be dealt with at the CMC. It is also open to any party (or the Court) at a CMC to suggest that a claim started in the usual way is suitable for the Shorter Trial scheme.

3.20 Parties who have agreed that their dispute is suitable for the Flexible Trials Scheme must set out their proposal and agreed directions in advance of the first CMC.

3.21 Prior to the commencement of any claim in the Circuit Commercial court the parties should given consideration as to whether the case is suitable for either scheme.

4. Communicating with the Court

E-Mail

4.1 Although there is no provision for the electronic filing of documents apart from at the London Circuit Commercial Court (see below), parties may communicate with the Court by e-mail where the Circuit Commercial Court concerned provides an e-mail address. Where a dedicated e-mail address is given in Appendix A to this Guide, it should be used in preference to any general court e-filing address. Any such e-mail communications should not be accompanied by lengthy documents which need to be filed separately. The size limit is 40 pages in total of normal typescript or 2 MB whichever is the smaller. Nor should evidence for a hearing be lodged in this way. For details of Court e-mail addresses, see Appendix A. All e-mails to the Court must be copied to the other parties at the same time.

4.2 In an appropriate case, the judge concerned may provide his own e-mail address so that the parties can communicate directly with him, for example in relation to the submission of skeleton arguments or on post-hearing matters. The judge may agree with the parties when they might use that address. The particular e-mail address provided must be treated as strictly confidential. Any communication to the judge must be copied both to the other parties and to the Court on its own e-mail address.

Telephone hearings and paper applications

4.3 Even where there is an application to be decided by the Court it may not be necessary to have a full oral hearing. See section 8, Applications, below.

5. Particulars of Claim, Defence and Reply

Form, content, serving and filing statements of case

5.1 Statements of case should be as succinct as possible. They should not set out evidence. They should be limited to 20 pages in length. The court will give permission for a longer statement of case to be served where a party shows good reasons for doing so. Any application to serve a statement of case longer than 20 pages should be made on paper to the court briefly stating the reasons for exceeding that limit. It will rarely be necessary to plead large parts of a lengthy document in the statement of case. If this is necessary the parts should be set out in a schedule not in the body of the case.

5.2 The requirements of PD16 paragraphs 7.4–8.1 (which relate to claims based upon oral agreements, agreements by conduct and Consumer Credit Agreements and to reliance upon evidence of certain matters under the Civil Evidence Act 1968) should be treated as applying to the defence and reply as well as to the particulars of claim.

5.3 Full and specific details must be given of any allegation of fraud, dishonesty, malice or illegality. Where an inference of fraud or dishonesty is alleged, the facts on the basis of which the inference is alleged must be fully set out.

5.4 Any legislative provision (including any provision of The Human Rights Act 1998 or the Convention), and any principle or provision of foreign law upon which an allegation is based should be clearly identified and the basis of its application explained.

5.5 If a defendant wishes to advance a positive case on causation, mitigation or quantification of damages, proper details of that case should be included in the defence or Part 20 defence at the outset

5.6 PD16.7 para.3 requiring a copy of the contract to be served with the Particulars of Claim in a claim based upon a written agreement should be treated as also applying to the defence, unless the claim and the defence are based on the same agreement.

5.7 But in most cases, attaching documents to or serving documents with a statement of case does not promote the efficient conduct of the proceedings and should be avoided. If documents are to be served at the same time as a statement of case they should normally be served separately from rather than attached to the statement of case. Only those documents which are obviously of critical importance and necessary for a proper understanding of the statement of case should be attached to or served with it. The statement of case should itself refer to the fact that documents are attached to or served with it.

5.8 All statements of case must he verified by a statement of truth.

Serving and filing particulars of claim

5.9 Subject to any contrary order of the court and unless particulars of claim are contained in or accompany the claim form, the period for serving particulars of claim is 28 days after filing an acknowledgment of service: rule 59.4.(c). The parties may agree extensions of the period for serving the particulars of claim. However, any such agreement and brief reasons for it must be put in writing and notified to the court, addressed to the Court's Listing Office and the court may make an order overriding any agreement by the parties varying a time limit: PD59 para.6.

5.10 Unless the particulars of claim are contained in a claim form which the Court is to serve, the claimant must serve the particulars of claim on all other parties. A copy of the claim form will be filed at the Court on issue. If the claimant serves particulars of claim separately from the claim form he must file a copy within 7 days of service together with a certificate of service: rule 7.4(3).

Serving and filing a defence

5.11 The defendant must serve the defence on all other parties and must at the same time file a copy with the court. If the defendant files an acknowledgment of service which indicates an intention to defend, the period for serving and filing a defence is 28 days after service of the particulars of claim, subject to the provisions of rule 15.4(2). (See 59.9(2) and also Appendix 9 to the Commercial Court Guide for cases where the claim form has been served out of the jurisdiction).

5.12 The defendant and the claimant may agree that the period for serving and filing a defence shall be extended by up to 28 days: rule 15.5(1). However, any such agreement and brief reasons must be in writing and notified to the court: PD59 para.6.2. An application to the court is required for any further extension. If the parties are able to agree a further extension, a draft consent order should be provided together with a brief explanation of the reasons for the extension.

Serving and filing a reply

5.13 Any reply must be served and filed within 21 days after service of the defence: rule 59.9. A claimant who does not file a reply does not admit what is pleaded in the defence and a claimant who files a reply that does not deal with something pleaded in the defence is not taken to admit it. A reply is necessary when the Claimant wishes to allege facts (or rely upon a legal provision or argument) which have not been pleaded in the claim. Accordingly, it should not be served simply to repeat what is pleaded in the particulars of claim. Proper consideration should be given to the question of a reply as soon as the defence has been served. The reply should be served before case management information sheets are provided to the Court. This will enable the judge to see all the pleaded issues before the Case Management Conference ("CMC") and will assist the parties in preparing for it. In some cases, more than 21 days may be needed for the service and filing of a reply. In such cases an application should be made on paper for an extension of time (agreed if possible) and for a postponement of the CMC.

5.14 Any reply must be served by the claimant on all other parties: rule 59.9(1).

Amendment

5.15 Although PD58 para.8 applies only to the Commercial Court, it (and section C5 of the Commercial Court Guide) should be followed in the Circuit Commercial Court. Accordingly, an amended statement of case should show the original text unless the Court orders otherwise. But amendments may be also be shown by using footnotes or marginal notes, provided they identify precisely where and when an amendment has been made. Unless the court so orders, there is no need to show amendments by colour-coding. If there have been extensive amendments it may be desirable to prepare a clean unmarked copy of the statement of case for ease of reading. However, a copy of the statement of case showing where and when amendments have been made must also be made available. All amendments must be verified by a statement of truth unless the court orders otherwise.

5.16 Questions of amendment, and consequential amendment, should wherever possible be dealt with by consent. A party should consent to a proposed amendment unless he has substantial grounds for objecting to it. A party which considers that an amendment is required should apply for it at the earliest opportunity. Late amendments (especially those sought shortly before, or at trial) should be avoided and may be disallowed.

6. Case Management in the Circuit Commercial Court

General principles of case management

6.1 The court will take an active role in the management of the case through to trial. Parties should be ready at all times to provide the court with such information and assistance as it may require for that purpose. They are also encouraged to ask the Court to decide applications on paper or by telephone where that is clearly appropriate and where the other party has sufficient time to respond.

6.2 The CMC is a key event in the life of a case. The Court will wish to deal with as many issues as possible at that stage to save time and costs and the parties must be able and willing to assist the Court to achieve this.

6.3 Where parties fail to co-operate with each other (for example in failing to agree reasonable extensions of time) or take disproportionate steps or create delay, they may be penalised in costs.

Fixing the case management conference

6.4 The Claimant must apply for a CMC within 14 days of service of the reply or confirmation by the Claimant that no reply is to be served in the case of a Part 7 claim, or within 14 days of service of the Defendant's evidence in a Part 8 claim, or within 14 days of notification of transfer by the receiving court. If the Claimant fails to apply for a CMC any other party may apply or the Court may order a CMC of its own motion. When the Court fixes the CMC it may give specific directions in relation to it which shall take precedence over any directions set out below.

6.5 Because all interlocutory applications and CMCs are dealt with by the judge, it is essential that practitioners do not seek to list the CMC or any other application before a District Judge or Master as this will lead to delay. Equally, as all Circuit Commercial cases are allocated to the multi-track, no allocation questionnaire need be filed. The document relevant to a case's management in the Circuit Commercial court is the Case Management Information Sheet, dealt with in paragraph 6.15 below.

6.6 The CMC will be held at a hearing in the usual way unless a different order is made. Any party may apply in writing not later than 3 clear days before the hearing for the CMC to be held by telephone and the Court will then decide on paper whether to proceed in this way or not.

6.7 Where a party is represented, a legal representative familiar with the case and who has sufficient authority to deal with any issues likely to arise must attend. In a heavy or complex case, the retained advocate should attend if possible.

Documents required for the cmc

6.8 Subject to any earlier order of the Court, not less than 7 days before the CMC the parties must file with the Court (a) a Case Management Information Sheet ("CMIS") in the form set in Appendix B and (b) an application notice for any application not covered by an order sought in the CMIS.

6.9 In addition, the Claimant (or other party applying for the CMC) shall also file and serve a case management file containing:

Part 3 The Circuit Commercial (Mercantile) Court Guide

- **(a)** statements of case;
- **(b)** a brief summary of what the case is about;
- **(c)** the list of issues;
- **(d)** the CMISs;
- **(e)** draft directions which should as far as possible be agreed with the other party and which may be based upon the template at Appendix C; such directions should also be e-mailed to the Court using the appropriate e-mail address contained in Appendix A;
- **(f)** a costs budget in the form set out in Precedent H annexed to PD3E;
- **(g)** a disclosure report;
- **(h)** Where expert evidence is sought, a document identifying the field of expertise and the pleaded issues to which it relates, the estimated cost of the expert and (if possible) their identity;

6.10 If there is any significant dispute likely to arise at the CMC the parties should also serve written submissions in relation to it, 2 clear days before the hearing and file them by e-mail at the relevant address.

List of issues

6.11 The list of issues is intended to be an agreed record of the principal issues of fact and law arising in the case and must be prepared before the CMC and after service of the reply (if any). It should be a neutral document to assist the Court and the parties in the management of the case, for example in relation to preliminary issues, the scope of disclosure, witness statements, or expert evidence. Accordingly, it should not be heavily drafted, negotiated or slanted. It is not a statement of case or a substitute for one. The parties must make every effort to agree the list of issues.

6.12 If there is genuine disagreement over the list of issues the parties should produce their own rival lists if possible using one document with the differences highlighted;

6.13 The list(s) of issues should be e-mailed to the Court at the relevant address prior to the CMC and any later hearing where they may be relevant;

6.14 The Court may order the list of issues to be refined or clarified at or after the CMC.

The case management information sheet

6.15 This is an essential aid to the understanding by the Court (and the other side) as to one party's assessment of how the case is expected to progress to trial, and its cost, along with the evidence to be called. Parties who fail to lodge it can expected to be penalised in costs in an appropriate case. It is in the form at Appendix B.

Costs budget

6.16 Rules 3.12 to 3.18 together with PD3E have introduced a costs management scheme. This applies to all cases in the Circuit Commercial Court except where the amount of money claimed in the claim form is £10m or more or the value of the claim is stated to be such. However the Court has a discretion to make larger claims subject to costs management or exclude smaller claims from it. Rule 3.13 and PD3E require the parties (other than litigants in person) to file and exchange costs budgets in Precedent H as directed by the Court and in any event 21 days before the first CMC and to file and exchange Budget Discussion Reports (preferably in Form R) 7 days before the CMC.

6.17 A costs budget is "an estimate of the reasonable and proportionate costs (including disbursements) which a party intends to incur in the proceedings" (see CPR Glossary). It is required in advance of the CMC so that the Court can consider whether or not to make a costs management order ("CMO"). Subject to paragraph 6.16 above, where costs budgets have been filed and exchanged the court will make a CMO unless the case can be conducted justly and at proportionate cost without one. Even in cases falling outside the scheme, the use of costs management should always be considered. The CMO is an important tool for the management of costs and the case generally.

6.18 A CMO is made when the Court either records the extent to which the costs budgets are agreed between the parties or where, in the case of a budget or part of budget which is not agreed, the court records its approval after making any appropriate revisions. When considering a costs budget for the first time, the Court may not approve the costs within any phase which have already been incurred. But it can record any comments on the proportionality or otherwise of such costs and take them into account when considering costs going forward. Incurred costs should where possible be allocated to the particular phase of litigation to which they relate. Nor may the Court at any stage retrospectively approve any change to the costs budget where the further costs have already been incurred. It is thus incumbent on parties to seeking approval for any variations before the relevant costs have been incurred. For the effect of a costs budget on the assessment of costs see paragraph 15.4 below.

The case management conference

6.19 At the CMC the Court will give such directions for the management of the case as it considers appropriate. It will consider actively the exercise of its case management powers set out in rules 1.4 (2) and 3.1 and those attending must be prepared to assist in that exercise and be in a position to provide the Court with all necessary information. While the parties need not themselves attend, it may be very advantageous for them and their lawyers for them to do so especially in a substantial case. In all cases, clients must be easily contactable by their representatives at the time of the CMC.

6.20 The Court is likely to give particular consideration to

  (a) whether any of the issues can be narrowed and if so how, and whether a split trial or trial of preliminary issue is appropriate;

  (b) whether further information should be provided by a party where it has been requested within a reasonable period but declined and the parties' legal representatives have been unable to resolve the issue;

  (c) the scope of disclosure, including electronic disclosure, and where relevant, a summary of the parties' discussions as to the disclosure and inspection of Electronic Documents (see paragraphs 10.5–10.6 below) and the use of information technology' in the management of documents generally;

  (d) whether expert evidence is necessary and if so whether it may be adduced by a single joint expert or if not, by the parties' experts giving their evidence concurrently;

  (e) the extent to which ADR has been considered or attempted;

Part 3 The Circuit Commercial (Mercantile) Court Guide

- **(f)** whether the case s appropriate for Early Neutral Evaluation;
- **(g)** whether the parties have co-operated with each over the management of the case thus far;
- **(h)** whether or not to make a costs management order under rule 3.15 and PD3E and if so what if any revisions are required to the parties' costs budgets where they have not been agreed.

6.21 Accordingly, the parties' representatives must be fully prepared and able, to discuss in detail with the Court the matters referred to above along with any other matters likely to arise. The aim of the Court, in all but the most substantial of cases, is to have one CMC only.

6.22 At the CMC, the Court may fix a trial date and pre-trial review ("PTR") (if appropriate). Parties must therefore have details of availability of witnesses and advocates to hand. Advocates must also be in a position to give a clear and reliable estimate of the length of trial.

6.23 The Court may also decide to fix a Progress Monitoring Date. If it does, it may after that date fix a further CMC or a PTR on its own initiative if no or insufficient information has been provided by the parties or it is otherwise appropriate.

6.24 The parties may not less than 7 days before the CMC submit agreed directions up to trial (in hard copy and by e-mail) and invite the Court to vacate the CMC on that basis. The Court will consider the position on paper and may vacate the hearing, order it to take place by telephone, maintain it or make any other appropriate order. Parties must assume that the hearing will proceed unless notified to the contrary.

6.25 Subject to the discretion of the judge dealing with the CMC, the Court may issue directions agreed and/or ordered at the CMC based upon the electronic version submitted beforehand. This may enable the directions to be issued and sealed at the conclusion of the CMC itself.

Further case management conference

6.26 In some cases it may be necessary to hold a second CMC. In others, the judge may of his own motion wish to discuss some aspect of the case with the parties and may require a telephone or oral hearing. The parties should be prepared to accommodate such hearings.

Compliance with court orders

6.27 Compliance with rules, practice directions and particular directions or orders made by the Court is part of the overriding objective. Serious sanctions may be prescribed by the rules or the Court for non-compliance. Applications by the party in breach for relief from such sanctions will be the subject of careful scrutiny by the Court.

7. Alternative Dispute Resolution

Adr generally

7.1 Business cases are often easier to settle than other disputes particularly when the relief sought is confined to the payment of money. Many businesses are able to settle a case by direct discussions or through their lawyers. If this does not work parties are encouraged to consider the use of ADR (such as, but not confined to, mediation) as an alternative means of resolving disputes or particular issues.

7.2 The settlement of disputes by means of ADR saves costs and avoids the delay inherent in litigation. It may also enable the parties to settle their dispute while preserving their existing commercial relationships and market reputation. ADR also provides parties with a wider range of solutions than those offered by litigation.

7.3 Lawyers should in all cases consider with their clients and the other parties concerned the possibility of attempting to resolve the dispute by ADR and should ensure that their clients are fully informed as to the most cost effective means of resolving their dispute.

7.4 Parties who consider that ADR might be an appropriate means of resolving the dispute or particular issues in it may apply for directions at any stage, including before service of the defence and before the CMC, for example to stay the proceedings pending mediation.

7.5 In any event, the Court will in appropriate cases invite the parties to consider whether their dispute, or particular issues in it, could be resolved through ADR, especially, but not only, at a CMC. Whenever

Part 3 The Circuit Commercial (Mercantile) Court Guide

there is a substantial application being heard by the Court the parties should be prepared to discuss ADR at the conclusion of the hearing.

7.6 The judge may, if he considers it appropriate, adjourn the case for a specified period of time to encourage and enable the parties to use ADR. He may for this purpose extend the time for compliance by the parties with any requirement under the rules, the Guide or any order of the Court. The judge in making an order providing for ADR, will normally take into account, when considering at what point in the pre-trial timetable there should be compliance with such an order, such matters as the costs likely to be incurred at each stage in the pre-trial timetable if the claim is not settled, the costs of a mediation or other means of dispute resolution, and how far the prospects of a successful mediation or other means of dispute resolution are likely to be enhanced by completion of pleadings, disclosure of documents, provision of further information under CPR 18, exchange of factual witness statements or exchange of experts' reports.

7.7 The judge may further consider in an appropriate case making an ADR Order in the terms set out in Appendix 3 of The Commercial Court Guide.

7.8 At the CMC the judge may consider that an order directed to encouraging bilateral negotiations between the parties' respective legal representatives is likely to be a more cost-effective and productive route to settlement then can be offered by a formal ADR Order. In such a case the court will set a date by which there is to be a meeting between respective solicitors and their respective clients' officials responsible for decision-taking in relation to the case in question.

Early neutral evaluation

7.9 In appropriate cases, and with the agreement of all parties the court will provide a without-prejudice, non-binding, early neutral evaluation ("ENE") of a dispute or particular issue. Any party may apply for an ENE and if a Circuit Commercial Judge considers that it is appropriate he will give such directions for its preparation and conduct as are appropriate. The judge who conducts the ENE will take no further part in the case, either for the purpose of the hearing of applications or as the judge at trial, unless the parties agree otherwise. An ENE

Part 3   The Circuit Commercial (Mercantile) Court Guide

may be conducted entirely on paper, or after a hearing (with or without evidence) although in general such hearings will not be expected to last more than one day. The Judge conducting the ENE will give his conclusion with brief reasons, either orally or in writing. Parties are encouraged to consider ENE as one form of ADR especially where they feel unable to settle the dispute without some formal indication as to where the merits lie, and hence what might be the result at trial.

7.10 Whether it is practicable to make an ENE order at any given Circuit Commercial court may depend on the judicial resources available there, given that the judge hearing the ENE may thereafter be unable to hear the case.

8.   Applications to the Court

Generally

8.1 Applications are governed by Part 23 and PD23 as modified by rule 59 and PD59.9 and 10. Any application for an order should include a draft of the order sought. Where possible an electronic version of the Order in Word should be submitted as well. Once an application has been issued by the Court copies will be sent to the party making the application for service, unless the Court has agreed to effect service. The Circuit Commercial Court is conscious of the time and cost of an oral hearing. Accordingly it is willing to consider hearing applications by video-link, telephone or on paper in an appropriate case. It is unlikely to do so in the case of an application for summary judgment/strike out, interim payment, security for costs, injunction (save where it is without notice and urgency dictates it) or other substantial application. The form of application notice enables the applying party to select which mode of determination it seeks, subject thereafter to the agreement of the Court. All applications may be submitted by CE-Filing and practitioners are encouraged to so do. See paragraph 3.3 above.

Time for service of evidence

8.2 The time allowed for the service of evidence in relation to applications is governed by PD59.9.1 and 9.2. Broadly, except in applications which are going to last more than half a day, evidence in support of an application is to be served with that application, evidence in answer is due within 14 days of service and evidence in reply within 7 days after that.

Applications without notice

8.3 All applications should be made with notice, even if that notice has to be short, unless a rule or Practice Direction provides that the application may be made without notice or there are good reasons for making the application without notice, for example, because notice might defeat the object of the application. Where an application without notice is otherwise appropriate and does not involve the grant of an injunction, it will normally be dealt with by the judge on paper, as, for example, with applications for permission to serve a claim form out of the jurisdiction, and applications for an extension of time in which to serve a claim form. But in any given case the judge may require the applicant to provide clarification or further information by telephone or at a brief hearing, or to serve the other party..

8.4 On all applications without notice it is the duty of the applicant and those representing him to make full and frank disclosure of all matters relevant to the application.

Expedited applications

8.5 The Court will expedite the hearing of an application on notice in cases of sufficient urgency and importance. Where a party wishes to make an expedited application a request should be made to the court on notice to all other parties.

Video-conferencing

8.6 Most Circuit Commercial Courts have facilities for video conferences. When an applicant wishes to have a matter heard in this way, it should say so in the application and explain why. The other parties should then indicate to the Court as soon as possible after being served whether they agree or riot, giving reasons. Even if the parties agree, the Court may still decide that a full oral hearing, or conversely a telephone hearing, is more appropriate. Information about each Court's video conferencing are in Appendix A.

Telephone hearings

8.7 If the Court agrees that an application may be dealt with by telephone, it will normally be for the applicant to arrange the telephone conference which should include the recording of the call.

Paper applications

8.8 Attention is drawn to the provisions of rule 23.8 and PD23A.11. If the applicant considers that the application is suitable for determination on paper, he should ensure before lodging the papers with the court that (a) the application notice together with any supporting evidence has been served on the respondent; (b) the respondent has been allowed the appropriate period of time in which to serve evidence in opposition; (c) any evidence in reply has been served on the respondent; and (d) there is included in the papers the written consent of the respondent to the disposal of the application without a hearing; or a statement by the applicant of the grounds on which he seeks to have the application disposed of without a hearing, together with confirmation that the application and a copy of the grounds for disposing of without a hearing have been served on the respondent and a statement of when they were served.

8.9 The parties may ask the Court to deal with certain matters relating to the management of proceedings in correspondence without the need to issue an application notice. For example, this may be appropriate where the issue is costs only or the working out of figures or particular orders, following a hearing, the timing of certain directions where their substance is already agreed or has been determined or the identity of a single joint expert or mediator. The party making this request shall copy its request the other party at the same time. Subject to any other direction of the Court, the other party shall then have two clear days in which to indicate to the requesting party and to the Court its consent or opposition to matters proceeding in this way. If the Court decides to proceed in this way, it will inform the parties and they shall then make their representations on the matter in issue as directed by the Court. The Court will then decide the matter and issue the appropriate supplemental order.

Bundles and skeleton arguments

8.10 An application bundle must be lodged with the Court 2 clear days before the date fixed for the hearing. The applicant should, as a matter of course, provide all other parties to the application with a copy of the application bundle. Appendix 7 of the Commercial Court Guide deals with in detail with the preparation of bundles.

8.11 Skeleton arguments must be provided by all parties. These must be lodged with the Court at least one clear day before the date fixed for the hearing together with an estimate of the reading time likely to be required by the court. Guidelines on the preparation of skeleton arguments are set out in Appendix 5 of the Commercial Court Guide. On some applications there will be key authorities that it would be useful for the judge to read before the oral hearing of the application. Copies of these authorities should be provided with the skeleton arguments. In any event, bundles of the authorities on which the parties wish to rely should be provided to the judge hearing the application as soon as possible after skeleton arguments have been exchanged.

8.12 Both the application bundle and the skeleton arguments are vital advance material for the judge who is to hear the application. If they are not filed, the hearing may be vacated or costs sanctions applied. If there is likely to be a problem with the delivery of the bundle, it is the responsibility of the applicant to inform the Court forthwith and to indicate when it will be filed. Equally it is the responsibility of Counsel to inform the Court if a skeleton argument cannot be filed on time, and why.

8.13 At any stage before the hearing of an application if it appears to the Court that the application bundle and/or skeleton arguments should be filed at an earlier stage it may issue directions to that effect.

8.14 If at any time either party considers that there is a material risk that the hearing of the application will exceed the time currently allowed it must inform the Court immediately. All time estimates should be given on the assumption that the judge will have read in advance the skeleton arguments and the documents identified in the reading list.

8.15 If it is found at the hearing that the time required for the hearing has been significantly underestimated, the judge hearing the application may adjourn the matter and may make any

special costs orders (including orders for the immediate payment of costs and wasted costs orders) as may be appropriate.

8.16 On any hearing expected to take up to one day, the judge is likely to assess summarily any costs which a party has been ordered to pay. Such assessments, and related costs matters are dealt with in paragraphs 15.5 to 15.7 below.

9. Injunctions

Generally

9.1 Applications for interim injunctions are governed by Part 25. They must be made on notice in accordance with the procedure set out in Part 23 unless there are good reasons for proceeding without notice. Except when the application is so urgent that there has not been any opportunity to do so, the applicant must issue his claim form and obtain the evidence on which he wishes to rely in support of the application before making the application.

9.2 On applications of any weight, and unless the urgency means that this is not possible, the applicant should provide the court at the earliest opportunity with a skeleton argument.

Without notice injunctions

9.3 If an injunction is sought without notice, the applicant will be expected the explain the basis for it. Any delay in seeking the injunction may prove fatal. Parties are reminded of the duty to make full and frank disclosure on such applications. If the injunction is granted, the Court will normally fix a return day within, not more than 7 days later. The applicant should endeavour to provide an electronic version of the order sought. It may then be possible for the Court to issue it (with appropriate amendments) at the conclusion of the hearing.

Fortification of undertakings

9.4 Where the applicant for an interim injunction is not able to show sufficient assets within the jurisdiction of the Court to support the undertakings given, particularly the cross-undertaking in damages, he may be required to reinforce his undertakings by providing security. This will be ordered in such form as the judge decides is appropriate but may, for example, take the form of a payment into court, a bond issued by an insurance company or a demand or other guarantee or standby credit issued by a first-class bank. In an appropriate case the judge may order a payment to be made to the applicant's solicitors to be held by them as officers of the court pending further order. Sometimes the undertaking of a parent company may be acceptable. Accordingly, any party seeking an injunction must come prepared to deal with the question of providing security.

Freezing injunctions and search orders

9.5 The practice of the Circuit Commercial Court is to follow the practice and procedure of the Commercial Court. See section F15.8–15.15 of the Commercial Court Guide. Standard forms of wording for freezing injunctions and search orders are set out in Appendix 11 thereto. They should be followed in the Circuit Commercial Court unless the judge orders otherwise. Accordingly, any draft submitted should be in the form prescribed by Appendix 11. Any departure from the standard form must be specifically drawn to the judge's attention at the hearing.

9.6 Parties are reminded that an affidavit, and not a witness statement, is required on an application for a freezing injunction or a search order. (PD25A para.3.1) and that the duty of disclosure is especially important in this context.

10. Disclosure

Generally

10.1 The court will only order such disclosure as is necessary and proportionate. Rule 31.5 (7) contains a list of different disclosure orders of which standard disclosure is only one. It is not to be regarded as the default option and in many cases a narrower and more tailored order will suffice. Usually, this will be disclosure of documents upon which each side relies together with a request of the specific disclosure which it requires from the other party. The Court may consider such a request at the CMC. The parties are required to state in their disclosure report and CMIS which particular order they seek and why.

10.2 If a party contends that standard disclosure is necessary and proportionate it must also set out the limits of any search required by such an order and why any wider such (for example for particular classes or categories of document) would be unreasonable (see rule 31.7).

10.3 It follows that a party's costs budget must reflect the particular disclosure order sought.

10.4 The parties are expected to discuss the appropriate disclosure order prior to submitting their disclosure reports and CMISs with a view to agreeing them subject to the approval of the Court. They should in any event be prepared to discuss with the Court at the CMC the proper scope of disclosure and how it, and the consequent inspection, might most appropriately be made This may include using information technology (for example CDs, DVDs or memory sticks) to exchange copy documents and to access them thereafter and at trial.

Electronic disclosure

10.5 This is governed by PD31B. The extensive use of information technology in business dealings makes this a particularly relevant provision for Circuit Commercial cases. Para. 5 (3) defines an Electronic Document as "any document held in electronic form. It includes, for example, e-mail and other electronic communications, such as text messages and voicemail, word-processed documents and databases and documents stored on portable devices such as memory sticks and mobile phones. In addition to documents that are readily accessible from computer systems and other electronic devices and media, it includes documents that are stored on servers and back-up systems and electronic documents that have been deleted. It also includes Metadata and other embedded data which is not typically visible on screen or a print out." Para. 7 requires parties' legal advisers to notify their clients of the need to preserve disclosable documents which include Electronic Documents. Failure to observe this requirement, so that, for example, important documents only emerge at trial, may have serious consequences including the adjournment of a hearing and costs orders against the defaulting party, which may be awarded on an indemnity basis.

10.6 The parties should also, prior to the first CMC, discuss any issues that may arise regarding searches for and the preservation of electronic documents. This may involve the categories of Electronic Documents within their control, the computer systems, electronic devices and media on which any relevant documents may be held, the storage systems and document retention policies, the scope of the reasonable search for such documents, the means by which the burden and cost of disclosure might be reduced and the other matters referred to in PD31B para.9. In general the parties should provide the court with an explicit account of the issues as to retrieval and disclosure of electronic documents which have arisen and where proportionality is in issue each party should provide the court with an informed estimate of the volume of documents involved and the cost of their retrieval and disclosure. They should also co-operate at an early stage as to the format in which electronic copy documents are to be provided on inspection. They should also consider the use of information technology in the conduct of the proceedings generally including the disclosure and inspection and/or copying of non-Electronic Documents- see paragraph 8 above.

10.7 Para. 14 requires the parties to submit before the first CMC a document summarising the extent of the parties' agreement on such matters. Where there is disagreement the Court will make the appropriate orders which may include the holding of a further CMC on disclosure and/or the completion of an Electronic Documents Questionnaire.

Specific disclosure

10.7 An order for specific disclosure under rule 31.12 may direct a party to carry out a thorough search for any documents which it is reasonable to suppose may adversely affect his own case or support the case of the party applying for disclosure or which may lead to a train of enquiry which has either of these consequences and to disclose any documents located as a result of that search: PD31A para.5.5. Specific disclosure is normally the subject of a separate application but the parties should be prepared to discuss at the CMC whether such an application is likely and if it is, whether any issue relating to particular documents can be conveniently dealt with at the CMC.

11. Witness Statements

Preparation and form of witness statements

11.1 Witness statements must comply with the requirements of PD32. In addition,

- **(a)** the function of a witness statement is to set out in writing the evidence in chief of the witness; as far as possible, therefore, the statement should be in the witness's own words;
- **(b)** it should be as concise as the circumstances of the case allow without omitting any significant matters;
- **(c)** it should not contain lengthy quotations from, or commentaries upon, documents;
- **(d)** it is seldom necessary to exhibit documents to a witness statement;
- **(e)** it should not engage in (legal or other) argument;
- **(f)** it must indicate which of the statements made in it are made from the witness's own knowledge and which are made on information or belief, giving the source for any statement made on information or belief;
- **(g)** it must contain a statement by the witness that he believes the matters stated in it are true;
- **(h)** it is usually convenient for a witness statement to follow the chronological sequence of events or matters dealt with (PD32 para.19.2). It is also helpful for particular topics covered to be indicated by the appropriate heading.

11.2 Witness statements which do not comply with the above may face sanctions from the court including the striking-out of the offending passages and adverse costs orders.

11.3 The copies of witness statements to be inserted into the trial bundle must be annotated with the trial bundle references of the documents to which they refer.

Fluency of witnesses

11.4 If a witness is not sufficiently fluent in English to give his evidence in English, the witness statement should be in the witness's own language and a translation provided. If a witness is not fluent in English but can make himself understood in broken English and can understand written English, the statement need not be in his own words provided that these matters are indicated in the statement itself. It must however be written so as to express as accurately as possible the substance of his evidence.

Additional evidence from a witness

11.5 A witness giving oral evidence at trial may with the permission of the court amplify his witness statement and give evidence in relation to new matters which have arisen since the witness statement was served: rule 32.5(3). Permission will be given only if the Court considers that there is good reason not to confine the evidence of the witness to the contents of his witness statement: rule 32.5(4).

Witness summonses

11.6 If a witness will not voluntarily provide a witness statement and agree to attend Court, the relevant party may wish to serve a summons for the witness to attend court or to produce documents in advance of the date fi for trial. A witness summons is issued by the Court at the request of the relevant party who must then serve it; but if the summons is to be served within 7 days before the trial, the permission of the Court is needed. See rule 34.2–34.7 and also rule 32.9.

Witness summaries

11.7 Where a party cannot obtain a statement from an intended witness, he may apply to serve a witness summary instead which summarises the evidence which will be given (for example following issue of a witness summons) or if not known, the matters on which the witness will be questioned. See rule 32.9.

Evidence to be given by video-link

11.8 A witness may give evidence by video-link or by other means other than oral testimony when present at the trial, if the Court permits, (rule 32.3). The Courts which have video-link facilities are listed in Appendix A. Parties seeking to use such facilities should make application at an early stage, preferably at the CMC and in any event no later than the PTR. Detailed guidance is at PD32 Annex 3 and section H3 of the Commercial Court Guide.

12. Expert Evidence

Generally

12.1 Any application for permission to call an expert witness or serve an expert's report should normally be made at the CMC when the party applying will be expected to have identified in advance the expert's field of expertise the issue to which the evidence relates, its cost and if possible the name of the expert..

12.2 However, the court will only make an order for expert evidence when satisfied that it is in fact reasonably required for the resolution of the case. The party seeking such evidence must demonstrate this by reference to the nature of the evidence to be given, the expertise of the proposed expert and the pleaded issues to which it is said to be relevant. Even if expert evidence is justified, in many cases this can be provided by a single joint expert (see below). If either or both parties seek a direction that each side is to have its own expert, this must be justified as necessary and proportionate. The court is unlikely to make such an order merely because both sides have agreed it.

12.3 The provisions set out in Appendix 8 to the Commercial Court Guide apply to all aspects of expert evidence (including expert reports, meetings of experts and expert evidence given orally) unless the court orders otherwise. Parties should ensure that they are drawn to the attention of any experts they instruct at the earliest opportunity.

Single joint expert

12.4 Such an expert may often be appropriate for example where the issue is self-contained or subsidiary or where it consists largely of testing or other analysis which can conveniently be done for all parties by one expert. The fact that the issue is complex or that one side has already instructed an expert does not necessarily mean that an order for a single joint expert is inappropriate.

12.5 When the use of a single joint expert is contemplated, the court will expect the parties to co-operate in developing, and agreeing terms of reference for that expert and his fees. In most cases the terms of reference will (in particular) identify in detail what the expert is asked to do, identify any documentary materials he is asked to consider and specify any assumptions he is asked to make.

Exchange of reports

12.6 In appropriate cases the court will direct that the reports of expert witnesses be exchanged sequentially rather than simultaneously. This may in many cases save time and costs by helping to focus the contents of responsive reports upon true rather than assumed issues of expert evidence

and by avoiding repetition of detailed factual material as to which there is no real issue. Sequential exchange is likely to be particularly effective where experts are giving evidence of foreign law or are forensic accountants. This is an issue that the court will normally wish to consider at the CMC. The Court will also consider whether it should provide at the outset for the service of supplemental reports where the initial reports were exchanged simultaneously.

Concurrent evidence

12.7 Para. 11 of PD35 provides for expert evidence at trial to be taken concurrently, that is to say with both experts in the witness box at the same time. This enables the judge and the trial advocates to receive the immediate view of both experts on a particular matter and the opportunity for the experts to make points to each other as well as answering questions. There remains the opportunity for the trial advocates to ask questions of the experts. In an appropriate case this procedure will lead to a saving of time and costs (for example by narrowing issues and avoiding repetition) and enabling the judge to have a clearer understanding of the real issues between the experts. Para. 11 sets out various forms of concurrent evidence and is accompanied by an extensive guidance note. Therefore, at the CMC or later hearing or at the PTR the parties and the judge will give careful consideration as to whether an order for concurrent evidence should be made.

Meetings of expert witnesses

12.8 The court will normally direct a meeting or meetings of expert witnesses before trial. This will normally follow the exchange of reports. However, in some cases it may be appropriate to direct an initial meeting of experts even before exchange of reports. This may narrow some assumed issues or ensure that both experts are addressing themselves to the precisely the same issues. Sometimes it may be useful for there to be further meetings during the trial itself.

12.9 The purposes of an experts' meeting are to give the experts the opportunity to discuss the expert issues and to decide, with the benefit of that discussion, on which expert issues they share or can come to share tire same expert opinion and on which expert issues there remains a difference of expert opinion between them (and what that difference is).

12.10 Unless the court orders otherwise, at or following any meeting the experts should prepare a joint memorandum for the court recording:

(a) the fact that they have met and discussed the expert issues;
(b) the issues on which they agree;
(c) the issues on which they disagree; and
(d) a brief summary of the reasons for their disagreement.

12.11 If the experts do reach agreement on an issue that agreement will not bind the parties unless they expressly agree to be bound by it.

Written questions to experts

12.12 Under rule 35.6 a party may, without the permission of the court, put written questions to an expert instructed by another party (or to a single joint expert) about his report. Unless the court gives permission or the other party agrees, such questions should be for the purpose only of clarifying the report. The court will pay close attention to the use of this procedure (especially where separate experts are instructed) to ensure that it remains an instrument for the helpful exchange of information.

Trial

12.13 At trial the evidence of expert witnesses is usually taken as a block, after the evidence of witnesses of fact has been given. The introduction of additional expert evidence after the commencement of the trial can have a severely disruptive effect. Not only is it likely to make necessary additional expert evidence in response, but it may also lead to applications for further disclosure of documents and also to applications to call further factual evidence from witnesses whose statements have not previously been exchanged. Accordingly, experts' supplementary reports must be completed and exchanged not later than the progress monitoring date and the introduction of additional expert evidence after that date will only be permitted upon application to the trial judge and if there are very strong grounds for admitting it.

13. The Pre-trial Review and Trial Timetable

13.1 Where a PTR has been ordered, the Pre-trial Check List (substantially in the form reproduced here as Appendix D) must be filed at Court not less than 7 days before the PTR.

13.2 If no PTR has been ordered, the Pre-trial Check List should be served 6 weeks before the trial date unless otherwise ordered. In such a case, the judge will consider the Pre-trial Check Lists and decide then

Part 3   The Circuit Commercial (Mercantile) Court Guide

whether to order a PTR. If he does not, he may on his own initiative give directions for the further preparation of the case or as to the conduct of the trial.

13.3 Where a PTR has been ordered it will be conducted by the trial judge whenever possible. The advocates who will appear at the trial should attend.

13.4 A PTR gives the Court the opportunity to review the case before the trial and the parties the opportunity to ventilate any remaining procedural issues between them. Failure by the parties to mention any matter which ought properly to be dealt with at this stage and which is left to trial may be taken into account when the Court at trial decides what order (including any order for costs) to make.

13.5 The Court will also revisit the time estimate for trial and consider the trial timetable. This should provide for openings, witness evidence, expert evidence and oral closing submissions, over the course of (he trial. The trial timetable should be submitted 2 clear days before the PTR.

13.6 The parties may not less than 7 days before the PTR request the Court in writing to vacate it on the basis that there are no issues which fall to be determined or that any such issues have been resolved by consent in the form of agreed directions submitted to the Court at the same time in hard copy and by e-mail. The Court will consider the position on paper and may vacate the PTR, order it to take place by telephone, maintain it or make any other appropriate order. Parties must assume that the hearing will proceed unless notified to the contrary.

14. The Trial

Trial bundles

14.1 The bundles of documents for the trial should be prepared in accordance with Appendix 7 of the Commercial Court Guide which contains an essential checklist. The number, content and organisation of the trial bundles should be approved by the advocates with the conduct of the trial. They should consist of files with 2 and not 4 rings.

14.2 Parties are reminded that apart from certain specified documents, trial bundles should include only necessary documents: PD39A para.3.2(11). Consideration must always be given to what documents are and are not relevant and necessary. Where the court is of the opinion that costs have been wasted by the copying of unnecessary documents it will have no hesitation in making a special order for costs against the party responsible.

14.3 The number, content and organisation of the trial bundles should be agreed in accordance with the following procedure, subject to any other direction of the Court:

(a) the claimant should submit proposals to all other parties at least 4 weeks before the date fixed for trial;

(b) the other parties should submit details of additions they require and any suggestions for revision of the claimant's proposals to the claimant at least 3 weeks before the date fixed for trial.

14.4 Preparation of the trial bundles should be completed not later than 2 weeks before the date fixed for trial. Parties are reminded of the requirement under PD39A para.3.9 to agree questions of authenticity and admissibility or summarise their disagreement.

14.5 It is the responsibility of the claimant's legal representative to prepare and lodge the agreed trial bundles: see PD39A para. 3.4. If another party wishes to put before the court a bundle that the claimant regards as unnecessary he must prepare and lodge it himself. Bundles should be lodged with the Court at least 7 days before trial. If bundles are lodged late, this may result in the trial not commencing on the date fixed, at the expense of the party in default. An order for immediate payment of costs may be made.

14.6 If oral evidence is to be given at trial, the claimant should provide a clean unmarked set of all relevant trial bundles for use in the witness box: PD39A para.3.10. The claimant is responsible for ensuring that these bundles are kept up to date throughout the trial.

Opening submissions

14.7 The Claimant's opening note should outline its case on the issues for trial, highlighting (by reference to trial bundle numbering) the key documents and providing a reading list for the Court with an estimate of how long pre-reading will take. The legal framework for the claim should also be set out although extensive legal argument or citation of authorities is not required at this stage. The Defendant's note should be similarly concise. The timing and mode of service of the notes will have been set at the PTR or by agreement between the parties and the Court. Under normal circumstances such notes must be provided at least 2 clear days before the trial and may be ordered to be sequential.

Opening speeches

14.8   The Court will usually permit a brief opening speech by the Claimant and a response from the Defendant. This gives the Court and the parties an opportunity to clarify any matters arising out of the opening notes and narrow issues if possible.

Applications at trial

14.9   If it is necessary to make an application for example in relation to evidence it should be made at the earliest point in the trial which may be during opening. Parties should not delay in making such applications on the basis that as the trial progresses they might become unnecessary.

Closing submissions

14.10 The form and timing of closing submissions will be decided in the course of the trial. The usual course particularly in the case of shorter trials, is that the advocates will be expected to make oral closing submissions, either immediately after the evidence has been completed or shortly thereafter. Unless the trial judge directs otherwise, the claimant will make his oral closing submissions first, followed by the defendant in the order in which they appear on the claim form with the claimant having a right of reply.

14.11 In a more substantial trial, the court may well require written closing submissions before oral closing submissions. In such a case the court will normally allow an appropriate period of time after the conclusion of the evidence to allow the preparation of these submissions.

15. Costs

Generally

15.1 See Part 44. The general rule is that the unsuccessful party will pay the successful party's costs but the judge may make a different order: rule 44.3 (2). Parties should note that their conduct during the proceedings may be taken into account in the ways set out in rule 44.3 (4) and (5). The judge may disallow the costs of, or make a costs order against, any party which has unnecessarily increased costs at any stage.

15.2 Circuit Commercial cases are often complex with a variety of different issues to be decided. Accordingly, the judge may have regard to the outcome on particular issues as well as who has succeeded overall; see rule 44.3 (4) (b).

15.3 The judge has the power to make a wide range of orders to give effect to the merits of the parties' position on costs, including ordering payment of a proportion only of a party's costs or in a fixed amount, or from or until particular dates: rule 44.3 (6).

The effect of a cmo

15.4 Where a CMO has been made and there is an assessment of the costs of the party awarded its costs ("the receiving party") on the standard basis, the court must have regard to that party's costs budget! and may not depart from it without good reason. This applies to both summary and detailed assessments. It is thus important for parties to keep their costs budgets up to date. See further paragraph 16.18 below.

Summary assessment of costs

15.5 The general rule is that if a hearing in the Circuit Commercial Court takes no longer than a day, the judge will assess the costs summarily. If a CMO has been made the Court is likely to assess summarily the costs in longer hearings including trials. If the application disposes of the whole claim, those costs may be summarily assessed, too: PD44 para.13.2.

Part 3 The Circuit Commercial (Mercantile) Court Guide

15.6 If a party wishes the Court to make a summary assessment of its costs, if the other side is ordered to pay them, it must provide statement of those costs with a detailed schedule, no later than 24 hours before the hearing: PD44 para.13.5. If this rule is not complied with, the judge may well decline to make an assessment and order that the costs be the subject of a detailed assessment in the usual way.

15.7 The Senior Court Costs Office's Guide to the Summary Assessment of Costs is at 48GP.17–48GP.56. Appendix 2 to the Guide contains a list of guideline hourly rates for solicitors across England and Wales, last updated in 2010. The Court is not bound to limit a party's costs to those rates but they are often regarded as a useful starting point. Cases justifying higher rates may be where the work has had to be done with real urgency or where the amount at stake or the complexity of the case, is substantial.

Payment on account of costs

15.8 Even if a summary assessment is not made, for example because of pressure of time or the nature or extent of the disputes over the costs incurred, or because the hearing has exceeded one day, the Court will usually order that a payment on account of such costs be made. See rule 44.2 (8). But if it is to do so, it will normally require a document which gives at least some detail as to how the sum claimed is arrived at. If a CMO has been made the Court is likely to order a payment on account by reference to the receiving party's costs budget..

Pro bono costs orders

15.9 If a party had legal representation which was provided free of charge (for example under the Bar Pro Bono Scheme or by the Access to Justice Foundation), the Court may order the other party to pay such costs as it would have ordered against it, had the first party's representation not been free of charge. It can assess such costs or order a detailed assessment in the usual way. The recipient is, however, not the first party but the Access to Justice Foundation. Such orders may not be made against those whose own representation is provided without charge or who are funded by the Legal Services

Commission. See s194 of the Legal Services Act 2007, CPR 46.7 and PD46 para.4.1.

16. Litigants in Person and Companies without Representation

16.1 Those bringing or defending claims in the Circuit Commercial Court are sometimes unable to afford legal representation or do not have it for some other reason. Such "litigants in person" require special consideration.

16.2 Where a litigant in person is involved in a case the court will expect solicitors and counsel for other parties to do what they reasonably can to ensure that he has a fair opportunity to prepare and put his case. The duty of an advocate to ensure that the court is informed of all relevant decisions and legislative provisions of which he is aware (whether favourable to his case or not) and to bring any procedural irregularity to the attention of the court during the hearing is of particular importance in a case where a litigant in person is involved.

16.3 Further, the court will expect solicitors and counsel appearing for other parties to ensure that they provide the various documents required for the management of the case and trial, even where the litigant in person is unwilling or unable to participate. If the claimant is a litigant in person the judge at the CMC will normally direct which of the parties is to have responsibility for the preparation and upkeep of the case management bundle. The court may also give directions relating to the costs of providing application bundles, trial bundles and, if applicable, transcripts of hearings to the litigant in person.

16.4 The Court itself will adopt such procedure at any hearing as it considers appropriate to further the overriding objective where a litigant in person is involved. This may include ascertaining from such a person the matters on which he should give evidence or be cross-examined or putting questions to him.

16.5 A litigant in person does not have to file a costs budget.

16.6 Litigants in person are reminded that if their case is in Birmingham, Bristol, Cardiff Leeds, Liverpool, London, or Manchester, they may

Part 3   The Circuit Commercial (Mercantile) Court Guide

obtain very helpful support before and during a hearing (though not extending to legal advice or representation) from the court's Personal Support Unit ("PSU"). See its website at: www.thepsu.org.uk and the individual contact details at Appendix A for those Court centres where the PSU operates. The other parties in the case should remind the litigant in person of this service at those centres if he appears to he unaware of it. The Court's experience is that the involvement of the PSU can be of great assistance to both parties, as well as the judge.

16.7 Litigants in person may also seek the assistance of a "McKenzie friend" who may sit alongside them in court and provide assistance such as taking notes or making quiet suggestions to them. If sought, permission for a McKenzie friend is usually given unless fairness or the interests of justice do not require it. It is less common for the court to grant a right of audience to a particular individual who is not otherwise qualified to act as an advocate although there is power to do so under paragraph 1(2) of Schedule 3 to the Legal Services Act 2007. It would be exceptional for the court to grant permission where the person concerned is unqualified but holds himself out as providing advocacy services. See generally section 13G in Volume 2 of the White Book.

16.8 Although rule 39.6 enables the Court to allow a company or other corporation without legal representation to be represented at trial by an employee, the complexity of cases in the Circuit Commercial Court may make that unsuitable.

17. Arbitration Claims

17.1 Applications to the court under the Arbitration Acts 1950–1996 and other applications relating to arbitrations are known as "arbitration claims". The procedure applicable to arbitration claims is to be found in Part 62 and PD62. The most common claims are (a) appeals on a point of law against the arbitration award where the parties have provided for this in the contract (b) applications for permission to appeal where they have not (c) applications to set aside the award for serious irregularity and (d) applications to enforce an arbitration award. Almost all arbitration claims are made under the Arbitration

Part 3   The Circuit Commercial (Mercantile) Court Guide

Act 1996. Only the Commercial Court, the Technology and Construction Court and the Circuit Commercial Court have jurisdiction to deal with them. The claims dealt with by the Technology and Construction Court will usually relate to construction or similar contracts. Part 59, which deals with the Circuit Commercial Court generally, applies to arbitration claims unless any provision in Part 62 says otherwise: rule 62.1(3). In general, the Circuit Commercial Court will apply section O of the Commercial Court Guide.

17.2 The automatic directions set out in PD62 para .6 will apply unless the Court has otherwise ordered.

17.3 Where the claim is for permission to appeal, the detailed procedure set out in PD62 para. 12 will apply. Sometimes a party also seeks to challenge the award on the grounds of serious irregularity. If so, both claims should be made in the same claim form. On receipt of the papers the judge will consider whether such claims should be dealt with together or separately and give appropriate directions or order a hearing to take place to discuss the matter further.

17.4 In the interests of saving costs and of proportionality the Circuit Commercial Courts may be expected to deal informally and robustly with some smaller arbitration claims which seem obviously misconceived.

17.5 Enforcement of awards is governed by rule 62.18. An application to enforce must be made without notice in an arbitration claim form, supported by written evidence and accompanied by two copies of the draft of the order required. If the Court gives permission to enforce the defendant will be given 14 days (more if outside the jurisdiction) to apply to set it aside and no enforcement will take place until the 14 days or longer period expires or any application to set aside is disposed of.